GOD'S CALL TO BE LIKE JESUS

LIVING A HOLY LIFE IN AN UNHOLY WORLD

David W. Kendall

GOD'S CALL TO BE LIKE JESUS:
LIVING A HOLY LIFE IN AN UNHOLY WORLD
by David W. Kendall

ISBN 0-89367-232-7

©1999
Light and Life Communications
Indianapolis, IN 46253-5002
Printed in the U.S.A.

C O N T E N T S

ACKNOWLEDGMENTS

The older I grow, the more aware I am of the contributions of others to my experience. If life is a garment God weaves from persons and circumstances at hand, then I must confess my deep gratitude for God's use of many special persons and circumstances. In varying ways, God is including threads from family, church, friends, and circumstance to weave a life of grace that I am learning to embrace completely and thankfully. For this I am grateful beyond words.

Special thanks to two friends, Professor Bob Green and Dr. Michael Hambley, who have read these pages critically and offered wise counsel. Their timely encouragement has meant far more than they realize.

And for Lavone I give thanks. Her love and support motivate me toward my best for the Kingdom!

David Kendall
McPherson, Kansas
Spring 1998

The writers of the Bible constantly stress the importance of holiness. God who is holy calls His people to be holy. In fact, the people of God are called "saints" or "holy ones" in Scripture.

Yet, unholiness abounds, inside and outside the church. Tragically, in both arenas, the same kinds of unholiness are rampant. In a two-week period, the incoming calls for pastoral care underscore what I mean. My journal for those weeks reports two failing marriages from within our congregation, one of those from verbal and emotional abuse, and the other because of hard-core pornography use. Both cases required that I spend many hours with these couples.

A few days later, I found out that one of our families was planning to leave the church. When I inquired, the husband assured me that I had heard right, and then fumbled to give me an adequate excuse. Now, I realize that sometimes a change of church is beneficial for a family. But, in this case, I felt that I was dealing with raw consumerism—they wanted to shop for something new, different, more exciting—or at least to see if it was out there.

Then I had another call about a disastrous marriage—not from our church—in which the husband was hopping from bed to bed. He and his wife were not believers, but over the course of the next few days, both of them recognized that they "were killing each other and messing up the kids big time." They needed something or someone, maybe God. "Could God help us sort out our feelings, take care of our guilt, give us a desire to 'do marriage right' and save our kids from becoming like us?" I assured them that He could, and then took a deep breath as I thought about all that God would need to do in their lives to create a healthy home.

Since these painful situations came on top of an already full schedule, you can see why I'd like to forget those two weeks. And yet, I can't, because of the glaring contrast between the Bible's call to holiness and the way so many people actually live, including those inside the church. I have no trouble believing what the pollsters are telling us—that a majority of Americans have made a "personal commitment to God." Most of these people claim to agree with traditional Christian beliefs that the Bible is the Word of God, Christ is the Savior of the world, prayer changes things, and the like. Yet, their responses demonstrate very little practical difference in the way they live from the unbelievers around them. When it comes to things such as basic honesty, faithfulness in marriage, use of time and money, their "believing" seems to make little difference in real life.

This kind of real life haunts me because it promises no good future. The brokenness I've described and see so often only leads to more brokenness. And the "easy believe-ism" of popular religion, even if called Christian, cannot heal the brokenness. But God can. He Himself is holy and He calls us to be holy. As we shall see, the root idea of "holy" is "different." Different from what? From the brokenness that is such a large part of modern life.

God has something very different in mind for His people. He calls us to a holy and whole way of life. If that sounds like good news to you, let's begin, by looking first at God Himself, the Holy One.

David Kendall

PART ONE

GOD'S HOLINESS

Apart from a clear sense of God's holiness, people and their societies lose a solid sense of the sacred and the faithful.

A renewal of our vision of God as holy will help us recover from this loss, and its tragic consequences.

Is Anything Sacred?

"I t was the best of times and the worst of times." With these words Charles Dickens began his classic *A Tale of Two Cities.* Certainly this sentence describes our modern world just as it did the world of Dickens' novel, for we see both good and bad things going on around us. Our focus determines whether we see the best or the worst.

But Dickens' sentence could describe our world in yet another sense. Whether life is the best or the worst depends on an individual's personal choice. One person decides what she sees is good, while another decides it's bad. Who's to say which one is right? No one, since every person must choose. There are no absolutes.

Our culture has adopted relativism as a foundational principle of life. "Beauty is in the eye of the beholder,"[1] we say. But now, so is truth and error, right and wrong, the sacred and profane. Each individual claims the right to choose.

But when we base our lives on the relativism in which everyone chooses, we're building on shifting sand. As an example, consider the question, "What is sacred?"

More specifically, consider how people today might answer that question compared with what their grandparents would have said when they were young.

When our grandparents were young, most people thought human life was sacred. Now our society supports an abortion industry that takes over a million lives every year. Sadly, most of these abortions serve as an extreme but effective form of birth control! Only about 3 percent involve situations of rape or incest, or of danger to the mother's life. And, one of every six women who has had an abortion claims to be an evangelical; these figures are reported by Focus on the Family.[2] At the other end of the lifeline, people like Dr. Jack Kevorkian and places like the state of Oregon champion the right of the suffering to end their own lives. They encourage doctors to help people kill themselves!

When our grandparents were young, most people thought marriage was sacred. Now many do not even consider divorce as odd, much less wrong. We can no longer even assume that the word "marriage" means a male-female relationship. Major companies—including Walt Disney, Microsoft, and Apple—offer medical coverage for the partners of homosexual employees.

When our grandparents were young, most people viewed sex as sacred. At least, they believed sexual relations should express the ultimate in loving commitment within the bonds of "sacred matrimony." Now sex sells, entertains, and offers a form of recreation. For some, sex is a god, the center and goal of living.

When our grandparents were young, a person's word and honor were sacred. Now research indicates that lying and cheating have become a way of life for many. In 1992 James Patterson and Peter Kim wrote *The Day America Told the Truth*. The book reported confidential surveys where most admitted that they regularly lied! These days no one will be impressed if you say, "You have my word on it!" Once you could buy most anything with such assurance. Now you can't rent a video! At best, modern folk regard the perception or image of honesty as sacred, but the reality may be another matter.

When our grandparents were young, religion, and especially Christian faith, was sacred. Now Christian faith competes with all sorts of spiritual options. In many public schools, Christian clubs are only one of several religious groups vying for student membership. Recently, the "Jesus Seminar" concluded that most of the portrayal of Jesus' life in the gospels reflects the bias of the early church. Mainline denominations find themselves bitterly divided on the question of ordaining practicing homosexuals.

You may be wondering, "What does all this have to do with me or with the Christians I know? We're not relativists!" Of course we're not relativists intentionally, but we must guard against its influence. Here are some situations that have made me wonder whether we are as free from relativism as we think.

- People in my own wonderful congregations have struggled with the guilt and lingering pain of aborting a child, and not always *before* they became Christians.
- Hardly anyone experiences shock when a professing Christian couple separates and divorces, as though the church has adopted a "no fault" divorce policy.
- Studies show that an alarming number of young people from Bible-believing churches are sexually active.
- Sunday ball games so easily claim the attention

and devotion of people who normally come to church.

■ Some Christian parents feel obligated to let their children play in sports leagues that require them to opt out of worship altogether, or to subscribe to a "worship-lite" schedule.

When individual choice in matters like these determines what is sacred, eventually we're left wondering, "Is anything *sacred* anymore?" Truly, unquestionably sacred? Why should we hold that human life, marriage, sexuality, honesty, and Christian faith claim sacred status? If so, on what basis can we make that claim? And how can we begin to recapture a proper sense of the sacred? To answer these questions, we must consider God's holiness.

THE SACRED MATTERS BECAUSE GOD IS HOLY

Our questions about the sacred are important, and not only because we lose so much when "nothing is sacred" anymore. The sacred matters because God reveals Himself as the Sacred or Holy One. Because God matters, the sacred, the holy, matters.

The Bible speaks clearly and often of holiness. Consider two striking examples. In the sixth century before Christ, God called Isaiah to serve as a prophet to His people. King Uzziah had just died, and chaos ruled politically, socially, and personally for the people of God. In that time of crisis, God gave Isaiah a vision of His awesome throne in heaven. Around God's throne he saw frightening but beautiful creatures serving the Lord, and calling to each other in thunderous voices, "Holy, holy, holy is the Lord Almighty; the whole earth is full of His glory" (Isaiah 6:3).

Make no mistake, those were desperate times for

the people of God. Big problems begged for solutions. But first the prophet had to begin, *as we all must,* with a vision of the holy. Indeed, God launched Isaiah's great work as a prophet with an affirmation of the sacred.

In the first century A.D., John the elder, writer of the Revelation, discovered the same truth. He found himself a political prisoner for his faith in Jesus, banished to the barren Island of Patmos, away from family and friends. But John had an inkling that God was about to do something big. God confirmed the inkling by revealing Himself and His plans. What God showed John became the book of Revelation.

John was "in the Spirit" one Lord's day, when he had the vision. Like Isaiah, he saw a throne room in heaven. At the center God was seated in dazzling splendor. Around God four living creatures constantly called out, "Holy, holy, holy is the Lord God Almighty, who was, and is, and is to come" (Revelation 4:8).

There was much wrong in John's world, but first things needed to come first. John's understanding of how God would deal with the mess of His world began with a vision of the holy. An affirmation of the sacred provided the key to God's plan! To make right what has gone wrong in our world, we must come to terms with the holiness of God.

GOD IS HOLY

In both the Old and New Testaments, the word "holy" means "different, separate, unique." To say that God is holy is to say that He is like no other, essentially different from other persons or things.

The first pages of the Bible show us God's holiness, even though the writer does not use holiness terms. Before anything was, God was. That's *why* the story opens, "In the beginning God ..." (Genesis 1:1). We can say that *only* of God. Then, day after day during the "week of creation" God said, "Let there be ..." and there was (see Genesis 1:3-31). That, too, applies *only* to God, for He stands "above" or apart from all that He created. In the story of creation, the writer always maintains the difference between God and the world, so that the Creator is never confused with the creation. That's another way of saying God is holy.

When we forget or reject God's holiness, it isn't long before we confuse God with other things or persons. That's what happened in the ancient world and it happens in our world. In ancient times many people thought the physical world, with its forces and cycles, *was* God. In our world people do much the same when they consult horoscopes, honor mother-earth, or seek guidance from the dead. They confuse God with what He has created.

Ancient peoples also thought of God, or the gods, in human terms. Reading their mythology is like watching Saturday morning cartoons. The superheroes are bigger and stronger than ordinary people, but still basically human. Understanding the gods in this way offered ancient peoples the hope of someday becoming godlike. Today, many self-help programs and new-age spirituality stress the god or godlike potential within each person. Both ancient and modern worlds confuse God the Creator with what He has created.

I sometimes wonder if we're not guilty of confusing God with creation when we think about God in buddy-buddy terms. Certainly God loves us. Jesus was friendly even toward "tax collectors and sinners" (Matthew 9:10-11; Luke 7:34). He invited His disciples to think of their relationship with Him as "friendship" (John 15:14-15). There is no doubt that God comes near and wants to establish an intimate relationship with us. But if He is only our friend or buddy, we risk lowering God to the level of other friends, and that can lead to spiritual disaster.

But God is not *only* our friend. He is also an awesomely powerful King and we must always understand ourselves as His servants. We need to remember both His friendship with us and His kingship over us. When God tells us to do something and we decide otherwise, we've confused God the Creator with His creation. When we confuse the two, we deny God's holiness. What's more, however, is that we are just a couple steps away from denying that *anything* is holy or sacred. Think it through. If God is like creation, then everything is basically the same, which means that *nothing* is sacred.

However, the Bible shows us that the sacred or holy does exist. Above all, the living God, Creator of all things, is holy. Because God *is* holy, He must hold a special or unique place in the universe and in our lives. Recapturing a sense of God's holiness is the key to restoring the sense of the sacred in our lives and world.

If God's holiness means that He is unlike other things and persons, how specifically is God different? And what sort of special place must God hold for us? These questions sharpen our focus as we ask, "What does it mean to say that God is holy?" In the remainder of this chapter, we will consider one answer to this and look at what it means for us.

GOD IS ABSOLUTELY INDEPENDENT

God created all things and persons. Therefore, everything that is owes its existence to God. In other words, God the Creator is independent and the creation is dependent.

Of course, most of creation cannot know this fact. Rocks, birds, caterpillars, even the most brilliant monkeys cannot know they depend on God the Creator.

If you have an aquarium in your home, you know that it requires a carefully maintained water-environment. When you take proper care of this watery world, the fish, algae, and underwater plant life thrive. All these life forms depend completely on the environment that someone else creates and maintains.

Think of it: the air we breathe, the water we drink, the food we eat, the clothing we wear, the work we do, the opportunities we have, the family and friends we enjoy—all that makes life rich, full, and satisfying comes as a gift from God. Understanding God's holiness teaches us not to take His gifts for granted, but to celebrate them as signs of our deep dependence on Him.

Although most of creation cannot understand this dependence, human beings can! Amazingly, we may know the God who made us and sustains us. Even pagans have sometimes grasped this insight. The Apostle Paul was quoting a non-Christian thinker when he said, "In Him we live and move and have our being" (Acts 17:28). How tragic if we seek to be independent from God. When we affirm His holiness, we identify God as the legitimate Lord and King of our lives.

God's holiness helps us understand the instructions He gives His people. We should not view God's law and word as arbitrary rules; they express God's holiness and help us understand our relationship of dependency on God. Since God is independent, He certainly has the right to show us how life works. But also, since we are dependent on God, we need the direction He gives in His Word.

Consider the Ten Commandments in this light. They

express God's holiness and lead us to live in dependence upon Him. The first four commands, which address the people's relationship with God, especially point to God as the incomparable Lord who calls us to live in a unique way. Let's look at how the first two commands serve His holiness. The first command is, "You shall have no other gods before (or "besides") Me" (Exodus 20:3). That makes perfect sense, since there are no other gods. As God's people, we must never regard another thing or person the way we regard Him. Further, every once in a while we should ask whether anything has taken a godlike place in our lives. Spouse, children, work, career goals, sports, hobbies, and many other things can become godlike for us, almost without our knowing. When they do, it always spells disaster. God's command helps us to enjoy a God-dependent life.

The second command is, "You shall not make for yourself an idol in the form of anything in heaven above or on the earth beneath or in the waters below. You shall not bow down to them or worship them; for I, *the Lord your God, am a jealous God"* (Exodus 20:4-5a, emphasis added). Since God is like no other, there is no way to represent Him accurately through created forms and images. The use of images as stand-ins for God will lead to a confusion between the Creator and the created. Most of us do not have to worry about idols as *physical* images. However, all of us tend to create *mental* images of God and His ways.

On December 31, 1984, eight-year-old Amy Jo entered the hospital for routine surgery to remove a cyst on her right hand. Her parents scheduled the operation during the holidays so Amy wouldn't have to miss school. "A simple procedure, in and out," the doctor promised. But after more than an hour in the waiting room, her parents became concerned. Then, several more hours threw them into a panic. Something was *very* wrong.

"Amy just wouldn't wake up," the doctor finally reported. Later investigation revealed that one of the machines malfunctioned, mixing the anesthetic ingredients in a deadly way. How tragic and unfair it seemed! For a long time Amy's parents questioned how God could be so cruel as to allow their little girl to die. Her death created a crisis in their faith because they had embraced a false image of God. *Their* image made it impossible for God to be real if little girls died in surgery.

Keeping the second command does not lessen the pain of losing a child, but it can guard us against a crisis of faith. God's instructions help us recognize His holiness and live a God-dependent life.

These two commands along with the other eight make supreme sense because God is holy. As the Holy One, He is absolutely independent and we are dependent. God is King and Lord; we are subjects and servants. God alone can show us how to live in ways that are good, right, and true. Far from being a burden, God's word of instruction, in the Ten Commandments and elsewhere in the Bible, reveals the way of life.

We must come to terms with God's holiness if we want to appreciate the life God has given us and then live it well.

IS THE SACRED A MATTER OF PERSONAL CHOICE?

In our world most people claim the freedom to define the sacred if and as they please. But, such "freedom" has brought tragic losses as human life is cheapened, marriages fail, and families disintegrate. Deep friendships and real intimacy become impossible. People no longer trust one another.

Precisely to our kind of world God says, "First things first!" We must catch a vision of the Holy One, for only when we affirm God as the sacred One, at the center of everything, will we get our bearings. Then the light begins to shine. Help comes.

Does it sound too simple to be true? After all, your marriage is strained. You feel depressed because nothing's going right. Circumstances and people have disappointed you. Some tragedy all but devastates you. You lose hope as the world goes mad! And God says, "Here's the way out: Recognize that I am holy!" Yeah, right!

But that *is* what God says to us, and not for the first time. In Isaiah's day society had gone from bad to worse. God diagnosed the problem this way, "Judah is morally and spiritually sick" (Isaiah 1:5-6). The legal system was not serving justice. The economy led the rich to oppress the poor. Religion had become big business designed to make evil appear good and good evil. Not surprisingly, crime was controlling the streets. Sexual freedom enslaved people to appetites that could not be satisfied. Enemies threatened to destroy the nation. And that was just the beginning (see Isaiah 1-5)!

God called Isaiah into this mess, commissioning him to give a word that would help his people. But Isaiah's mission began when he encountered and recognized God as the Holy One (Isaiah 6:1-13). It's the same for us. We cannot receive God's help apart from a realization of His holiness.

We must start by affirming God's holiness because all our human problems trace back to a denial of His holiness. Remember, God's holiness identifies Him as the Creator. As such, He is independent, the legitimate King of all.

When we rebel against God as King and Lord, nothing works well or right, and eventually, everything falls apart. Only God, the Holy One, can put it all back together. He begins to do this when we acknowledge Him as the Holy One. That's why God says, "First things first!"

When we acknowledge the Holy One as the center of our lives, we begin to learn two important lessons. First, *we learn to live in humility and gratitude.* When the Holy One draws near, we confess our unholiness and unworthiness. Isaiah saw the Lord and nearly fell apart, pronouncing woe upon himself. He realized he was not fit to be in God's presence and, by rights, should not have survived the experience.

Similarly, when John the elder saw his vision of God's holiness, he fell on his face, as though he were dead (Revelation 1:17). In the presence of the Holy One, we realize how unlike God we are, and the difference threatens us.

But wonderfully, God reaches out to those who are humbled in His holy presence. God responded to Isaiah's woe and cleansed his unclean life and lips (Isaiah 6:5-7). God picked John up off the ground and caused him to stand (Revelation 1:17-18). He does the same for us! Despite our unworthiness, God loves us and draws us into His holy presence. In response, we learn to live with a sense of humility and gratitude. We don't deserve the good things God does in our lives, but we are deeply grateful.

Second, *when we acknowledge the Holy One at the center of our lives, we learn to live with a spirit of surrender.* In fact, our surrender to God becomes "standard operating procedure" for us. After all, the Holy One *alone* is independent and we are dependent. Our well-being hinges on God having His way. Therefore, we give up our claims to independence. We offer ourselves and our situations to God. As we listen for God's direction, we learn what is good, right, and true. Then we look to God for *His* power to live life *His* way.

We do *not* have the freedom to decide for ourselves what is sacred. When we claim this freedom we make the sacred a hostage of personal preference or whim. The tragic outcome of this "hostage situation" can be seen all around us.

In fact, however, God is the Holy One. His independence as Creator and Lord of all, and our dependence on Him, will help us recapture and embrace the sacred. We begin by surrendering to Him in humility and gratitude.

Is Anyone Trustworthy?

N ot long ago the *New York Times* News Service published Lena Williams' "Adultery: 'Thou shalt not' or moral realism?" Williams notes that nobody praises adultery these days. Certainly most people would say it's wrong. Still, surveys suggest that adultery has increased over the past twenty years. In the 1970s, 25 percent of women and 50 percent of men admitted having at least one affair while married. In the 1990s these figures have jumped to 40 percent of women and 65 percent of men.

Even if the precise figures are debatable, the trend is alarming. In 1950 actress Ingrid Bergman had an affair with director Roberto Rossellini, from which a child was born out of wedlock. The Congress of the United States actually denounced these two for their infidelity. As a result, Bergman fled Hollywood! Today British royalty confess infidelity as a form of comfort for their miserable marriages, and they are swamped with letters of sympathetic support. This tolerant attitude toward unfaithfulness supposedly signals "moral realism," but what a high price such realism demands! It raises the question, "Can you trust anyone these days? And, if not your husband or wife, then whom?"

Try to imagine a world where no one trusts anyone.

- One morning your radio alarm clock goes off. You hear a cheery voice announcing the news: "This just in, during the night terrorists poisoned the town's water supply. The Centers for Disease Control in Atlanta advises that without treatment most people will soon become violently ill and die. Anyone who has had a drink during the night should proceed directly to the hospital." Panic sweeps across town. But, then, the panic becomes anger when it turns out to be a practical joke!

- Your doctor prescribes something to treat your symptoms, but you can't trust the pharmacist to give you what the doctor ordered!

- Your baby begins to have a seizure. You panic and call 911. Nobody comes!

- The restaurant people taint the food in a way you can't taste!

- The Uni-bomber becomes the Omni-bomber as everyone gets a kick out of mailing bombs. Opening the mail is a blast every day!

Can you imagine what such a world would be like? On some days we have to wonder if we're not even now building that kind of world.

And yet, I often see encouraging signs. One of my habits as a pastor is to visit the nursing homes in our town. I don't suppose I ever see anything more moving and wonderful than a husband or wife faithfully caring for a disabled partner. I think of one gentleman whose wife has Alzheimer's Disease. Over the last few years she has come to the point where she no longer recognizes him. When he visits, her condition keeps her from appreciating his care. Her bodily functions have slipped from her control. She will grow worse and perhaps live on for years.

Meanwhile, he also ages. His arthritis makes it more difficult to get around. Yet, every day he comes to visit her. He talks sweetly and lovingly with her, waits on her, wheels her around, feeds her, puts her to bed. And why does he do these things? More than fifty years ago this gentleman promised, "For better or for worse; in sickness and in health, so long as we both shall live." When he said those words, he had no idea what lay ahead for him and his bride. But he made a commitment, and he keeps it to this day!

What a remarkable model of faithfulness and loyalty! He's a man you can count on. Perhaps the people in your life have blessed you by their faithfulness—parents, husband or wife, children, friends, colleagues. As you think of them, you praise God for their remarkable goodness to you.

But that's just the point—they are remarkable, and increasingly rare. We're impressed by this loving husband's commitment and care because so many husbands would do something different under similar circumstances. All around us husbands abuse or abandon their wives and children, leaving them with years of pain to overcome. Perhaps you, or someone you know, experiences pain from the unfaithfulness of others. Our world prompts us to wonder if we can trust anyone. Are there some commitments we can absolutely count on?

GOD'S HOLINESS MEANS ABSOLUTE FAITHFULNESS

In the Bible God is called "holy." The most basic meaning of this term is "different" or "unique." Indeed, the difference between God and all others is infinite. In chapter 1 we tried to grasp the infinite difference between God and all else by saying God is absolutely independent. As the Creator of all, God is the only One who can claim independence. Everything and everyone else depends on God.

Here's another way to express the infinite holiness of God: God does not change. That doesn't mean He is old-fashioned or behind the times. Rather, it means He is consistent and reliable and absolutely faithful. *He* can be counted on, even if everyone else disappoints us.

From day one God demonstrated His faithfulness in dealing with people. In the beginning, He made people and placed them in a world that worked well. God Himself said it was "very good" (Genesis 1:31). It was good because God provided for all their needs. The first couple enjoyed plenty of good food, companionship, and something worthy and meaningful to do.

But, like little children, Adam and Eve thought they could do better. They decided to reject God and His holiness and be independent. People ever since have followed their example. They try to establish their own lives in their *own* way.

What do you do when rejected and offended by another? When you're told to "get lost"? When people twist your good intentions? When someone hurts you?

The relatives of the little victim screamed into the camera, "We want him to fry!" They insisted that even though Thaddeus Tyler was only sixteen, he would have to pay for getting his kicks by firing into the Jansen household in a drive-by shooting. Tyler's "kicks" killed three-month-old Nicole as she nursed at her mother's breast. Nicole's family wanted justice—and more. When others offend us we almost automatically want to respond in kind, even if the offense is minor. When someone cuts us off on the highway, spreads a bad word about us, criticizes us unfairly, steals our girlfriend—we want to pay them back!

But God is different, or holy. He made us and continues to care for us, even when we reject Him. He wants what is good for people and works to make it so.

Therefore, even with the sting of rejection still fresh, God made clothing for rebellious Adam and Eve (Genesis 3:21). He promised that the bitter results of their rebellion would not be final, that there would be a way out (Genesis 3:15). So, God called Abraham to father a people who would bring blessing to all families of the earth (Genesis 12:3). God delivered those people from slavery in Egypt. He gave them His word of instruction, the Law, to guide them in the good and right way. Then, since no one was perfect, God designed a system of sacrifice. When His people did something wrong, this allowed them to restore their relationship with God.

God's faithful commitment to His people brought them into the promised land. But even there, they rejected God and His ways (see Judges; Psalm 106). Of course, their rejection of God resulted in judgment. They suffered defeat by their enemies. Eventually they lost their homeland, and the survivors had to live in a hostile, foreign land.

Still, God did not give up on His people, but remained faithful. And, at the right time, God sent His own Son, Jesus, into the human family. The One who is unlike us became like us. The absolutely Independent One became dependent so that people could see God's holiness and faithfulness in human terms.

But, people in Jesus' day remained true to form and thought they could do better than God. Once again, they rejected God by rejecting Jesus and crucifying Him on a cross.

God allowed this. Because He is holy, God went to the limit and beyond for *our* good, when Jesus died. But then He raised Jesus from the dead and now, in love, He woos us to come to Him, to be His and to let Him work in our lives for our good.

And God is not finished yet! He has made some promises about how this world will end and how people will fit into the picture. Even now He's moving us toward a time when all His promises find fulfillment. Because God is holy, absolutely faithful, this time will certainly come. Then God's holiness will be central to all of creation, in a new heaven and new earth. There will be no need for the sun, moon or stars, no need for a temple or special place to meet with God, because He, the Holy One, will be at the center. At that time everything will be as God wills, absolutely! Anything working against His best wishes for His world will be forever gone. No tears, no death, no curse. All will be well because God is absolutely faithful (see Revelation 21-22).

CAN YOU TRUST ANYONE!

Are there some commitments you can count on, no matter what? Because God is holy, the answer is YES! No matter how hurtful people have been to you, no matter how unfairly life has treated you, no matter the brokenness of your experiences or the unhealthy things you may have done to cope with it all, God's plan to make it right still stands, and God's plan includes *you*! You can be certain of this because God's holiness means *He* can be counted on. Consider how this works in our lives.

Suppose one day that dear woman in the nursing

home with Alzheimer's Disease wakes up. As her right mind returns, she looks into the eyes of her husband, and understands. She says to herself, "For years this man has faithfully and lovingly cared for me in my weakness and illness. I didn't even know he was there. I was hardly aware of my needs, and couldn't do anything about them, but he knew and cared!" What do you suppose would happen next? Can't you just imagine her eagerly and lovingly seeking her husband's embrace? And, certainly, together they would experience a beautiful oneness and deep intimacy.

Something like that happens to us when we "wake up" and truly understand who God is and what He has done for us. God is holy and independent of us. Yet, He desires us, pursues our best interest, and cares for us. He cared even when we were so out of it that we didn't know what was going on. When we were in a kind of sinful stupor, unable to see straight, and clueless about our condition, God was absolutely faithful. He loved us, died for us, drew us to Himself.

When all this sinks in, when we wake up to these facts—if we ever truly do—we will want to be enfolded in His embrace. We will eagerly surrender to His loving intentions for us. Without doubt, we will want to follow His lead to be and do what is good, right, and true. Then we will begin to experience a beautiful oneness and deep intimacy with God!

In a world where trust is often scarce, here is God's answer. In absolute faithfulness to us, He seeks to draw us into an intimate love relationship. Within that relationship He, the absolutely faithful One, begins to make us faithful and trustworthy. As we live in His embrace, He makes us people of integrity.

Indeed, lack of integrity explains why we can

hardly count on anyone these days. Our talk does not translate into walk, even when our intentions are good.

Remember Peter's sad performance just before Jesus' crucifixion? Jesus had set a somber mood among the disciples, telling them He would soon suffer the betrayal, denial, and desertion of His dearest friends. Peter stiffened his back courageously and protested, "Not I! These others (his fellow disciples) may desert you, but I signed on for the long haul. Even if I must die with you, I'll never deny or disappoint you!" (see Mark 14:27-31). Peter meant well, but we know what happened.

We all wrestle with integrity, trying to make good on our best intentions. Most of us have vowed to live a victorious Christian life, establish a more consistent devotional life, serve the needs of others, work on our marriage, listen more carefully to our children (or parents), witness to a neighbor—all with the best of intentions. But we've failed at some point, or entirely. When we're honest, we know how impossible these things are without help from God.

When the absolutely faithful One draws us into His embrace, He becomes the center and focus of our living. His faithfulness draws our public and private lives together, and makes them one in Him. Then our intentions get translated into action. Others depend on our word. The conflict ends between what we should be and actually are, and what we should do and actually do.

Some question whether our world needs "holiness." In fact, the very word "holy" can raise strange and unattractive images that hardly seem relevant for a modern world.

And yet, when we listen to what God tells us in His word, the relevance of holiness becomes clear. When we lose a sense of the sacred, we are just a step away from losing everything. The world becomes a place where the reliable and the trustworthy disappear.

The good news is that God reveals Himself as the Holy One. When He is at the center He restores a sense of the sacred to us and He becomes the solid basis for rebuilding a sense of trust so necessary for meaningful relationships. He invites us to realize our dependence on Him and to receive the blessings *He* offers and *we* can count on.

PART TWO

HUMAN
HOLINESS

*When we recognize God as the Holy One,
we may have contrary reactions.
On the one hand, we understand
our unholiness and unworthiness,
our brokenness and alienation in the
presence of God. The distance between
divine and human becomes painfully clear.
Yet, on the other hand, we also begin
to understand who and how we were
meant to be. Seeing His divine holiness,
we long for the Person whose image
we were made to bear. To recognize the
Holy One is to be both repulsed and attracted.*

*The painful distance between us
and God repulses. Yet, our brokenness
and our awakening to the person
we might be attracts us.*

*God responds to both our repulsion and
attraction. He overcomes the painful distance
between us and Him through forgiveness
and then draws us into deep oneness
with Himself. Divine holiness creates and
sustains human holiness when God's presence
becomes an everyday reality in our lives.*

CHAPTER THREE

Who Wants to Be Holy?

All through the Bible God calls His people to be holy. This suggests it really is possible to live a holy life. But why would we want to be holy? Most people, even some inside the church, do *not* place "holiness" in their top ten priorities. I think I understand why.

The very word "holy" often brings bizarre behaviors to mind. For some "holy" means "holier than thou," just like Brother and Sister Piffelsnort who believe they are better than most. The Piffelsnorts never miss an opportunity to witness to their superiority. Indeed, they seem to have a special gift of "self-promotion."

In certain parts of our country, the "holy" handle snakes and drink poison as proof of their faith! In other places, "holy" transmits images of the sour, stiff, stuffy, stingy, and somber. A "holy" person will be stand-offish, inhibited, prudish, fearful, and joyless. "Holy" may also label the religiously weird or odd. "Holy rollers" gather for services only to fall on the floor and utter animal-like sounds. It's enough to make the "unholy" shudder. If "holiness" means any of this, who needs it?

Being "holy," however, has nothing to do with

such things. When the Bible says we may be holy, it's announcing good news. Consider three reasons why. First, suppose we could be all we were meant to be. Wouldn't that be good? Actually, you and I were made to be holy. When we are holy, as the Bible understands holy, we are what God means us to be. Second, suppose we could be like Jesus. Wouldn't that be good? Is there a more inviting person in history? The great Mahatma Gandhi of India once reportedly said, "I am not a Christian because I've never met anyone like Jesus. If I did, maybe I'd become one." How good it would be for the world to be full of people like Jesus. Third, suppose the world were full of people just as they were meant to be and just like Jesus. Wouldn't that help to solve most of our problems? Our world desperately needs holiness, rightly understood and powerfully real in human life. In truth, there could hardly be better news than this: we may become holy.

Yet, we must be careful about our definition of "holy," because God alone is the Holy One. That means He is incomparable, with no equal. We can never be holy as God is. No matter how saintly we may become, there will always be an infinite difference between God and us.

Still, the Bible applies this word "holy" to people. *How can people—ordinary human beings, so totally beneath God, people like us—be called "holy"?* Let's see how the Bible answers that question.

THE BIG PROBLEM

Imagine Adam and Eve one second after God finished creating them. At that time everything was perfect and God said, "It is very good" (Genesis 1:31). Even then, however, under the most ideal circumstances, only

God was the Holy One. At their most innocent, Adam and Eve were not holy as God is holy.

But that was a small problem compared to our big problem—we do not have ideal circumstances. Strictly speaking, since God alone is holy, we are not holy because we are not God. But worse still, we are not holy because we are sinful!

Almost from the beginning, the human race decided to reject God's holiness. The first temptation challenged God's holy character: "God knows that when you eat of it your eyes will be opened, and *you will be like God, knowing good and evil"* (Genesis 3:5, emphasis added). The serpent suggested there was no real difference between God and us that a little forbidden fruit wouldn't cure. When Adam and Eve gave in to the temptation, they tried to be more like God than He made them to be. They were rebelling against God's rule as Lord of creation, thinking they could improve on His world.

But Adam and Eve's rejection of God hardly brought improvements. Instead, rebellion against God became a way of life for their children. This rebellion, in turn, has brought ruin to everything and everyone. Once they rejected God's holiness, nothing worked as it was meant to. The world of nature changed forever. The human person suffered distortion in mind, body, spirit, and emotions. No relationship in life escaped the effects of sin.

Like ripples in a pond, the first couple's "No" to God's holiness has shaped every person's life. The Apostle Paul explained this to Christians in Rome. Adam, head of the human household, made a bad choice that has brought pain and suffering to the whole family. As "children of Adam" we never "live down" the powerful im-

pact of Adam's misdeeds. Instead, all of Adam's children, including us, tend to do what Adam did (see Romans 5:12-21). Just as small children eventually walk
and talk and gesture like their parents, and just as they
develop the same habits and adopt the same attitudes,
so we become like our first parents.

Unfortunately, some of us have had better opportunity than others to understand the pain of this common human reality. A parent may have abused us or
become addicted to some substance. Or, maybe suffered
a severe emotional disorder. Often we discover that our
grandparents suffered in the same ways, though perhaps not as severely. Now we battle it, too. The cycles of
misery and defeat, passed from generation to generation, provide us a painful parable of what has happened
to the whole human family.

When we come into this world, therefore, we are
inclined or programmed for rebellion against God. We
will seek any way but His. What seems "natural" or "normal" to us has little in common with what God has
planned for us. We don't naturally recognize God as Creator and King, so we try to live a God-free life. And
where does that lead us? Since God determines the good,
right, and true, we lose our moral and spiritual bearings
if we attempt a God-free life. When we are convinced
that we can define the moral and spiritual for ourselves,
we become intensely centered on self. We value people
and things as they serve our own self-interest. We are
loving, kind, generous, and faithful when it advances
our own cause.

As we peel back the layers covering modern life,
we see that self-centeredness is ruining so many marriages, families, and communities. When the Bible speaks
of human nature as sinful, it refers to this "program-

ming" we've received from Adam.

We are not holy because we are not God. Far more seriously, however, we are not holy because we are sinful and deeply damaged by our rebellion against God. And the damage touches every part of us.

THE AMAZING FACT

Despite this damage done to ourselves, we still may be "holy." God finds ways to share His holiness. In the Bible we read of people, places, and things that are called "holy." In both Old and New Testaments God describes His people as "holy" and God judges them when they are not. The writer of Hebrews even says, "Without holiness no one will see the Lord" (Hebrews 12:14). It seems clear that people, along with places and objects, may share in the holiness of God. But, how?

God's presence makes people, places, and things "holy." When God comes near, persons and things do not remain the same.

Moses was wandering in the desert near Mount Horeb tending his sheep when, unexpectedly, he saw wisps of smoke in the air. As he came near he could see a bush on fire, but it wasn't burning up. He came even nearer until God called, "Stop! Do not come any closer. Take off your sandals, for the place where you are standing is holy ground" (Exodus 3:5). That patch of wilderness soil became holy *because God was there.* In time, Moses himself became a totally different person because God was with him. God's presence makes places and people holy.

Likewise, the Temple of God in Jerusalem was "holy." But its holiness did not come from its materials or the way it was built. Rather, God chose to visit and dwell in the Temple as in no other place on earth, and

God's presence made it holy. If God left the Temple it would no longer be holy, and that's exactly what happened later. The people of God sinned repeatedly, and finally God judged them by withdrawing His presence. When the Temple lost its holiness, invaders destroyed it.

These examples teach us that when God comes near to things, places, and persons, they begin to share His holiness. Probably you have had personal experiences that have brought this truth home to you, even if you didn't relate it to holiness. In a worship service, for example, when God makes His presence known—perhaps through a special ministry of music, in moments of silent prayer, or when the truth of the Word grips your heart—you've sensed God making the sanctuary or the moment different or holy. When you first committed your life to Christ, you *knew* God had come to live within you, and *you* were different. Indeed, much of your life changed. As you were experiencing the close presence of God, He was sharing His holiness with you! Simply put, if we live close to God we live a holy life. And when we live a holy life, we may expect two consequences.

■ First, *we are able to view ourselves and our human condition clearly.* In God's presence we see ourselves for who, and how, we are. The Prophet Isaiah experienced this in the Temple. God came near and he cried out, "Woe is me! I'm ruined, doomed. I am unclean in lips and life, and so are my people" (Isaiah 6:5). In the light of God's presence we can judge how our lives match or clash with God's character.

Peter had the same experience one day when Jesus called to him after a disappointing night of fishing, "Let down your nets for a catch." Peter's expertise as a fisherman told him it would be foolish to do so, but he obeyed because Jesus seemed to be a man of authority. When he did, the catch of fish nearly broke the nets. But Peter's response catches us off guard. Instead of celebrating his success, he fell at Jesus' feet and said, "Go away from me, Lord; I am a sinful man!" (Luke 5:1-8). Peter suddenly realized that Jesus is God, and in the presence of God, who is holy, he could see his own unholiness. Indeed, in God's holy presence we easily recognize thoughts, attitudes, actions, and reactions that do not match God's. Of course, we must then make a choice between God's way and our own.

About three years ago I went to a conference with hopes of being encouraged and renewed in my pastoral ministry. I was in need of a fresh touch from the Lord! When the conference began, I would have explained my need by telling you about some folks in the church who seemed picky and easily distracted from truly important things. *I* felt that they were majoring on minors and minoring on majors, thus blocking what God wanted to do in the church. So I prayed, "Lord, touch me, fill me, but whatever You do, by all means straighten *them* out!"

The Lord *did* touch me in a wonderful way. During the opening service God's Spirit invaded the sanctuary of my heart, and I knew I was in the awesome presence of the Lord. But while my spine still tingled and my heart raced with excitement, all of a sudden I saw my own attitudes as God saw them.

To my utter surprise, the Lord gently but powerfully showed me that I had been just as distracted as anyone in the church. In my mind, the Lord replayed several recent encounters with my daughter, reminding me of my irritation that her activities were inconvenienc-

45

ing me. No, it was more than irritation, it was anger! Anger enough to keep her from sharing with me her recent commitment to the Lord!

In a burst of painful insight, I realized that my irritation and anger over driving her around town kept her from sharing the best news of her life. Even worse, I had put myself in a position where I couldn't help her take important spiritual steps. I who had prayed for the Lord to work in her life, and I who had mentally cast stones at others in the church—I was in the wrong! I saw so clearly that I was the one who needed to be changed by God. When we are in His holy presence, God helps us to see our condition so that He may draw us closer and make us like Himself.

■ Second, *when we begin to live in God's presence and share His holiness, we are also called to serve.* In God's holy presence, we see that God works in all sorts of ways for the good of people. As we live in His presence, we are not only drawn to *be* like God, but also to *do* what God does in the world. That was the experience of Moses. Encountering God in His holiness gave him something to do, even though he didn't feel at all qualified (see Exodus 3). That was also the experience of Isaiah. He saw how unlike God he was, but God helped him so that before long, he heard himself praying, "Lord, I'm here. Send me. Use me. I'll serve!" (Isaiah 6:8). Peter's response matches the others. When he fell before Jesus confessing his sinfulness, Jesus reassured him and promised he would soon be fishing for people (Luke 5:10).

That's also the way it worked with me. In the opening session of that conference, once God's holy presence revealed where I was not like God, I was moved to repent and to trust God to change me. Then

I realized there were some things I must do because of the deepened sense of God's holy presence. Throughout the rest of the conference, the Lord showed me that I needed to repair the damaged relationship with my daughter, celebrate her commitment to the Lord, and pledge to support all God was doing in her life. Then, I had to make a full confession to my church family and *lead* them in seeking first God's kingdom and *His* righteousness.

The next Sunday morning, as I shared these things with my church family, God's Holy Spirit moved among us. In His holiness God visited us and many moved into a deeper relationship with the Lord. I was the first one to the altar! When we live in the presence of the Holy One, we will receive a servant's heart, and God will use us.

When God is present in our lives and we share in His holiness, we *see* where we do not match His character. We are drawn to be like Him and to *do* what God does in the world around us. Who we are and how we live begin to look "God-like."

But what about that big problem? How can we really be like God and do as God does when we are *sinful?* What can be done about the unholiness that seems so natural to us?

THE WONDERFUL GIFT

Jesus is the "gift of holiness." The God who is totally unlike us became like us in Jesus. Though His holiness put Him totally out of reach, He stooped down to our level. We can see what holiness looks like and how it behaves by watching Jesus. That's how we know that those unattractive and bizarre views of holiness are wrong. Jesus was not like that.

We begin to be holy people by joining ourselves

to Jesus and following Him. Our initial steps in following become the first steps in a holy life. That's what happened to Peter and the other disciples. He called them and, in following Him, they became different or holy people. As they walked with Jesus, they began to do and say things as never before. They went places they'd never visited and related to people and circumstances in new ways. What made them different? Being with Jesus, the Holy One. When He was with them, and they with Him, they were holy.

Of course, they were not perfect! They still needed God to work powerfully in their lives. God had to deal with their rebellion and sinfulness, and to heal the wounds of their past lives. But, becoming new or holy people—increasingly like Jesus in character and lifestyle—*began* when they determined to join Jesus' movement. That's how it begins with us too. And that's why most people feel as though things are different when they commit their lives to Jesus for the very first time. Things *are* different. Now they are walking through life with Jesus, which means never being the same again.

Indeed, in Jesus' ministry God's gift of holiness becomes complete. Jesus came to break the stranglehold of our rebellion against God. His death and resurrection open up a new way to be and to live. On a human level, we belong to Adam's "dysfunctional" family, doomed to repeat the same cycle of rejecting God and living for self. But in Jesus God gives us a new family where that cycle is broken. In our new family we find freedom from rebellion and self-centeredness and a freedom to be and to live in God-like ways.

48

WHO WANTS TO BE HOLY?

Nobody in their right mind wants to handle snakes, drink poison, or withdraw into weirdness and oddity. Nobody wants to become stiff, sour, or sad. And nobody really wants to be "holier than thou." God doesn't desire this for us either.

But most of us want to be "the way we were meant to be." Most feel the attraction of a Jesus-like life and would desire to be like Him. And almost everyone would agree, to be like Jesus and to be as we were meant to be would be good, not only for us but for our world. God also agrees.

That's why God calls us to be holy and then shows us how. Whenever God is present, persons, places, and things begin to share His holiness. Jesus is God with us, calling us to follow Him and base our lives on what He does for us. His death and resurrection repair the damage done by our sinful rebellion against God. As we trust Jesus and walk with Him, He fills us with His own Spirit, His *Holy* Spirit. His presence within us drives out whatever doesn't match His holy love. He inspires us to please Him in our daily lives and empowers us to pursue His plans in our world.

How May We Be Holy?

We have seen that God calls us to be holy. Even more, God assures us we may be holy. Not weird and not "holier than thou," but like Jesus. Jesus is God's presence with us and within us. And, God's presence in our lives makes us holy. But how does it happen? How does God move us from being like we are to being like Jesus?

Let me tell you about John and Candace. During their college years John fell in love with Candace and pursued her affections. The pursuit came easy for John, who was outgoing, fun loving, and good looking, always "the life of the party." For Candace, however, John's pursuit made life uncomfortable, because she was shy, reserved, and thought of herself as rather plain. Candace was the wallflower at the party, and she couldn't believe someone like John would be interested in her.

So John had his work cut out for him. He would have to be very creative to get her attention and convince her of his love. He showered her with flowers regularly. Once Candace returned to her room from class to find it filled with balloons. Then John commissioned Candace's friends as special messengers to tell her of his love. Finally, when he rented the sky-writing plane, she got the message. A year later John and Candace married.

In the years that followed, John and Candace had two daughters, moved to a major metropolitan area, and began a successful small business. The girls made their parents proud, and Candace began to come out of her shell. She believed in her God-given abilities and felt a deepening life partnership with John.

Then, one evening, everything fell apart with a phone call. Candace answered and a woman asked for John. Somehow it didn't feel right, and the more Candace thought about it, other questions came to mind about what she had seen and sensed in recent months. It took several days for the story to surface fully. John had enrolled in a graduate program and in one of his classes had met a young woman. One thing led to another until "business trips" became cover for a rendezvous between lovers. John's unfaithfulness devastated Candace, their girls, their home, and their faith. Both had been followers of Jesus for most of their lives.

Eight hundred years before Jesus' birth God told His people that He too felt devasted. God was an absolutely faithful partner to His people, but something went wrong with the marriage. His people left Him for other lovers. So God called the Prophet Hosea to model the pain God felt and the response God would make. What a tough assignment! "When the Lord began to speak through Hosea, the Lord said to him, 'Go, take to yourself an adulterous wife and children of unfaithfulness, because the land is guilty of the vilest adultery in departing from the Lord.' So he married Gomer daughter of Diblaim, and she conceived and bore him a son" (Hosea 1:2-3).

As expected, Gomer proved unfaithful. She aban-

doned Hosea for other lovers and, eventually, her unfaithfulness brought deep pain to herself as well as to
her husband. Perhaps you know from personal experience the devastation of a marriage shattered by adultery.
You understand the pain and the hopelessness of
Candace, of Hosea, and of God.

Indeed, God tells us, "That's the way it is between Me and you, my people." In our natural state,
we are painfully separated from God and at odds with
Him. Even though God made us for Himself, so that
our well-being depends on a loving and holy relationship with Him, we have broken that relationship. The
pain and brokenness of Candace and Hosea offer a
parable of our unfaithfulness toward God. *Can a
relationship so badly damaged be repaired?* Can it ever
again be holy? If so, how?

GOD TAKES ACTION FOR US

God refuses to settle for pain and brokenness. Instead, He pursues us. He seeks us where we are, arrang-
ing or rearranging our circumstances, working through
them, around them, or sometimes against them, to get
our attention and draw us to Himself. God announced
His intentions through Hosea, "Therefore I am now going to allure her; I will lead her into the desert and speak
tenderly to her" (Hosea 2:14). Then He spoke directly to
His unfaithful people:

> "In that day," declares the Lord, "you will call Me
> 'my husband'; you will no longer call Me 'my
> Master.' ... I will betroth you to Me forever; I will
> betroth you in righteousness and justice, in love
> and compassion. I will betroth you in faithful-
> ness, and you will acknowledge the Lord" (Hosea
> 2:16-20).

God responds to our unfaithfulness by taking action that will bring us into a special "holy" relationship with Him, despite *our* unfaithfulness. Ultimately, this divine response to human sin led Jesus to die on the cross. The Epistle of First John tells us, "This is love: not that we loved God, but that He loved us and sent His Son as an atoning sacrifice for our sins" (1 John 4:10). To be sure, if we love God, it is because "He first loved us" (4:19).

God's response to the brokenness of our relationship with Him makes possible a new relationship of love. A favorite hymn says it well:

> I sought the Lord, and afterward I knew
> He moved my soul to seek Him, seeking me;
> It was not I that found, O Savior true,
> No, I was found of Thee.
>
> Thou didst reach forth Thy hand and mine enfold;
> I walked and sank not on the storm-vexed sea;
> 'Twas not so much that I on Thee took hold
> As Thou, dear Lord, on me.
>
> I find, I walk, I love, but, O the whole
> Of love is but my answer, Lord, to Thee!
> For Thou wert long beforehand with my soul;
> Always Thou lovedst me.[1]

God always makes the first move, seeking to woo us and win us to a relationship of love and intimacy. We need to appreciate more than we do the wonder of God taking action for us. Perhaps we're tempted to think that, because God is great and mighty, what He has done is easy. Yet, consider three huge barriers standing between God and us.

■ The barrier of a broken heart, for one. Imagine

the pain Candace felt when John betrayed her. Recall the rejection you have felt in the past, the heartbroken-ness. "Heartache" seems an understatement when de-scribing the soul-deep anguish from such betrayal. Now imagine God, who is infinite in ability to feel pain and rejection. Surely the most devastating human brokenheartedness only begins to approach God's. Yet, He pursues us!

■ There is also the barrier of unjust rejection. It's painful to be rejected under any circumstances. But the sting reaches deeper when the rejection comes in re-sponse to love. John could claim no innocence or ex-cuse for his unfaithfulness. Likewise, Gomer's aban-donment of Hosea had no legitimate basis. In both cases, it was just plain wrong. Their partners had been mod-els of loyalty toward them. Similarly, we are in the wrong when we reject or ignore the God who made us. We repay a million undeserved kindnesses with blatant re-bellion. Imagine it, even in our rebellion God contin-ues to give us good things and the ultimately good thing, "While we were still sinners, Christ died for us" (Romans 5:8). Despite our unjust rejection of God, He pursues us!

■ The third barrier is our hard-heartedness, in-sensitivity, and denial. Probably Gomer could "justify" her unfaithfulness. If you could ask her she might cite some factors which seem to make wrong appear right. John did the same with Candace. "If only she had been this way or that, then I wouldn't have been attracted to the other woman." We do the same thing with God: "If only this hadn't happened, if only God had not allowed it, if I could just get a break, then maybe I would take God more seriously." It's amazing how often the guilty will try to make those they've offended responsible for their offense. Of course, such insensitivity and self-justification make the barrier higher between those who are separated. They also deepen the pain. Sadly, we have all played that game with others and with God.

Yet, God pursues us! What good news! He refuses to give up on people and takes action on their behalf. He sent Hosea to reclaim his unfaithful wife, "Go, show your love to your wife again, though she is loved by another and is an adulteress. Love her as the Lord loves the Israelites, though they turn to other gods" (Hosea 3:1). It's in the nature of God to come to where we are, to be there for us and draw us to Himself.

All these loving intentions of God came to full expression in Jesus. John put it like this, "The Word became flesh and made His dwelling among us" (John 1:14). God identified with us, stooped to our level in order to relate to us, as we do with our little children. Luke makes a major point of this by noting that Jesus was called "friend of tax collectors and sinners," people with the most sinful reputations (see Luke 7:33-34; 15:1-2). Jesus was not friendly toward sin, but toward people whose sin broke God's heart. He openly welcomed them. In fact, He came "to seek and save" them (Luke 19:10). At all costs, Jesus sought to close the gap between sinful people and a holy God. As the Apostle Paul declared, "God was reconciling the world to Himself in Christ" (2 Corinthians 5:19). That is, powerfully at work making peace between God and us.

But what about those enormous barriers—the broken heart of God and His rightful outrage over our unjust rejection of His kindness? Our rationalizing and self-justifying before Him? We could never deal with these barriers we've built. It requires divine demolition, which

God has done for us. Jesus died to destroy the barriers.

> Remember that at that time you were separate from Christ, excluded ... without hope and without God in the world. But now in Christ Jesus you who were once far away have been brought near through the blood of Christ (Ephesians 2:12-13).

God has taken the pain of our rejection and the offense of our insensitivity toward Him and nailed them to the cross. So far as God is concerned, the way to Him is now clear and open. He calls to us, wooing us into a holy relationship with Him.

WE MUST WELCOME A LOVING RELATIONSHIP WITH HIM

If God "proposes," we should accept. In order to do this, however, we need to first acknowledge the barriers. To be sure, God has dealt with them through Jesus, destroying them in His cross, clearing the way for us to know and love Him. But we must acknowledge what God has done.

The barriers are real. Each of us must recognize, "I have broken the heart of God. He knows me best and, therefore, has the least reason to love me. Yet He loves me the most. I have caused Him God-sized pain. Then I've made things even worse by trying to excuse myself and even blaming God." Recognizing the barriers and the pain they've caused is called "confession." Unless we admit the barriers, we can never appreciate fully the good news that God has removed them. If we truly confess the barriers, we will renounce them and turn away from all that breaks the heart of God. This turning away is called "repentance." When this One who has sought us out and taken action for us enfolds us in His forgiveness, a new and holy relationship begins.

57 = PAGE 42

What an amazing and powerful gift: God's forgiveness. Sometimes we seriously underrate it. Perhaps we place such a high premium on holiness, on the "deeper things of God," that we treat forgiveness as a small gift, merely preliminary to the real gift, holiness. It's easy to be confused by cultural misconceptions of what forgiveness means. One common error holds that forgiveness means "indifference." God pats us on the head, "There, there, that's okay!" Another misconception suggests that forgiveness means "denial." "You didn't mean it; no harm done." A third mistake is to make forgiveness a form of "indulgence." "Love is never having to say you're sorry."

In truth, however, receiving forgiveness from God requires that we "get real." Our offense against God wasn't okay. It was tragically, fatally wrong. It brought great hurt to God, to others, and to us. We *did* mean it. And the outcome required a supreme sacrifice, the death of Jesus. God's forgiveness is nothing less than a miracle that moves both ways between God and us. God's deep love flows toward us as He removes the painful barriers separating us from Him. But, then, when God forgives us He also gives us the capacity to love Him, deeply and passionately, with all that we are. This new love for God signals the holy life.

GREAT FORGIVENESS LEADS TO GREAT LOVE

Once a Pharisee invited Jesus to a dinner party. As He often did, Jesus accepted the invitation and joined a number of other guests at the Pharisee's table. We imagine a cordial dinner with stimulating conversation. But then everything changed, as a woman came to the place where Jesus reclined. For any woman to do this would have been shameful and disruptive. But this woman was known all over town as especially sinful. She came weeping convulsively and carrying a jar of perfume. She bathed Jesus' feet with her tears, dried them with her hair, kissed them with her lips, and anointed them with her perfume. Everyone watched in stunned silence. No doubt some of the other guests thought she was having an emotional breakdown. The Pharisee, however, concluded Jesus was neither a prophet nor holy. A *prophet* would know what sort of woman she was, and a *holy* man would not let her touch him.

But the host and guests were wrong, as Jesus explained through a parable. This woman, like a debtor who had been forgiven an enormous debt, could not help herself. She simply had to respond with a lavish display of love. Her great love demonstrated the great forgiveness she had received. In contrast, the Pharisee, who had no awareness of the gift of forgiveness, loved little (see Luke 7:36-50).

When God forgives us, He draws us near so that we begin to know this One who loves us supremely. That new relationship gives us the confidence that all is well between God and us. We are freed from fear or dread of being in God's holy presence and we begin to love the One who first loved us. Our love relationship with God makes us different or holy.

That's the way it worked with John and Candace, eventually. John's unfaithfulness brought the deepest pain to her and built up the highest barriers between them. Humanly speaking, there was no hope. But Candace was no longer a wallflower. She had become a woman made strong by God's forgiving love. Despite John's devastating rejection, God made her secure in His love and in His promise to care for her. Candace dared to trust that forgiveness could become the basis for a whole new kind of relationship. Not all at once, but no less surely over time, she remained open to John and loved him again.

Don't misunderstand. Candace didn't indulge or tolerate John's unfaithfulness. Hers was a tough love that suffered the pain of betrayal and then dared to reach out again. Then, for his part, John had to face the truth about himself and his conduct. He had to feel Candace's pain, and that of his children. Patiently and painstakingly he had to rebuild the trust and reestablish their confidence in his love. Eventually it happened and, amazingly, they now enjoy a deeper and more joyful relationship than before.

Candace opened the way for this to happen through the gift of forgiveness. John's acceptance of her gift began an entirely different relationship. In just the same way:

- When we face honestly the huge barriers that have separated us from God,
- When we feel the pain and hurt we have caused God and others,
- When we grasp the incredible truth that despite our poor track record God still reaches out to us, removes the barriers, and wants to embrace us in love, and
- When we reach back to accept His gift of love, then a new, different, holy relationship with God begins!

Holiness Is Oneness with God

There is life after the honeymoon. Once the excitement of the wedding and reception fades and you return from the honeymoon, you begin to make a life together as husband and wife. All the wonderful potential of marriage, "life's happiest and holiest relationship" your ceremony said, lies ahead of you. And you want to make the most of it, experiencing what it means to be "one flesh."

In the same way, once God has forgiven us and we begin to enjoy a new relationship with Him, we soon discover that we have a lot to learn about ourselves, God, and our relationship with God. We have a long way to go before we experience deep oneness with God.

My wife and I were engaged a year and ten months before we said, "I do." Let me share our story. I arrived on the campus of a small Christian college something of a love-starved puppy. High school had disappointed me socially, mostly for lack of opportunity. When I became a serious believer, I determined I would date and marry a girl who shared my commitment to following Jesus. Unfortunately, however, my small church didn't have many. I dated all three of them, twice, but my efforts proved useless. Then, a new pastor came to our church with a family full of girls. Surely it was a godsend, I thought. In the four years they served our church I went through the whole family of daughters, but my most valiant attempts led nowhere.

You can understand how I hit that small Christian college campus in a deprived condition that severely impaired my common sense. I felt more or less obligated to date every girl in sight who seemed serious about following Jesus. Three months of tiresome effort left me worn out and disillusioned. I even began to wonder if God had called me to the single life.

Then I met Lavone. Very soon we knew we were meant for each other. We shared common interests and values. Our conversations lasted long into the night and covered the most important subjects. We felt that special attraction—a chemistry—between us. So far as I was concerned, no other girl could ever compare.

But perhaps you can imagine how hard it was to wait twenty-two months to get married. And then how wonderful it was when August 16, 1975 arrived and we said, "I do." Clearly, we had a marriage made in heaven.

Whenever I work with couples preparing for their wedding, I always tell them, "You don't really know what you're getting into!" And I speak honestly from our experience. Lavone and I had a wonderful courtship, engagement, and wedding. We knew God meant us to be together and we gave ourselves to each other in love.

But it didn't take long for us to discover how little we knew about ourselves or living as "one flesh." Here's a brief rundown on the lessons. I discovered things about myself I hadn't shared with Lavone because even I didn't know them. I learned how much I like to do things "my way." That made me hard to live with. Without even trying, I offended her! Regularly I carried over routines and practices from my former days of singlehood. Often her tears told me how much this hurt. And I didn't communicate very well. Talking was no problem, but making connection with her was. My ears worked unreliably, and sometimes not at all.

At first these discoveries sent me into shock. We had a marriage made in heaven, I thought. We were in love. But we could be murder on each other. The road to oneness seemed long indeed. We now know that's the way it works in any relationship, including our relationship with God.

WE BEGIN WITH A LOVE RELATIONSHIP

The Bible uses the imagery of courtship and marriage to describe how God relates to us and makes us holy. He presents Himself as a faithful suitor who woos us and wins us as His bride. Truly, that is the marriage made in heaven.

God desires and pursues us, but not because He needs us. God is not love-starved or needy, like I was. Rather, we need God and were made for Him. Likewise, God does not pursue us because He finds us attractive and inviting as we are naturally. No, we have not treated Him very well at all. At the least, we have ignored Him, pretending He doesn't exist or doesn't matter. In different ways we have all rebelled against God and tried to live independently. As a result, we have offended Him.

To be sure, this imagery is not perfect. But realizing its imperfections only increases our wonder that God chooses to relate to us as a groom to his bride. Unlike any romance we've ever known, God desires and pursues us simply because He loves us and wants what is best for us. But there's nothing simple or easy about His love. Jesus *died* for us out of love, going to the limit and beyond, to draw us to God and establish a love relationship with us. For no good reason other than costly, sacrificial love, God claims us as His bride.

When we begin to understand what God has done, and when He convinces us He does really love us that much, we say, "I do." We commit ourselves to Him. Just as God claims us, we claim Him. The past, with all the barriers that had kept us from God, is swept away. Our forgiveness from God begins a relationship that promises oneness with God.

But on the way to oneness we discover a lot about ourselves we never knew before. We learn that some of the ways we think, feel, and act grieve God. With God in our lives, we now see that many of our assumptions and natural responses displease Him. Communication with God challenges us. We like to talk to Him, but we have a hard time listening so that we are in tune with Him. As we grow in our relationship with Him, all these discoveries present us with a choice.

When we understand more fully what it means to belong to God, we have to decide if we will continue to pursue this love relationship. Since it is a *love relationship*, God will not coerce us or force Himself on us. But He does lead us and empower us to make the right choice. He draws us to oneness.

Therefore, when we learn that something in our lives does not please Him, we must deal with it. That's a choice only we can make, yet we don't make the choice completely on our own. God lovingly leads us and empowers us to deepen the relationship He has established with us. By following His lead, we will enter into oneness with Him. In the Bible we see examples of this basic choice to pursue oneness with God. Let me share three of these.

WHOM WILL YOU SERVE?

Then Moses went up to God, and the Lord called to him from the mountain and said, "This is what you are to say to the house of Jacob and what you are to tell the people of Israel: 'You your-selves have seen what I did to Egypt, and how I carried you on eagles' wings and brought you to Myself. Now if you obey Me fully and keep My covenant, then out of all nations you will be My treasured possession. Although the whole earth is Mine, you will be for Me a kingdom of priests and a holy nation.' These are the words you are to speak to the Israelites."

When Moses went and told the people all the Lord's words and laws, they responded with one voice, "Everything the Lord has said we will do." Moses then wrote down everything the Lord had said.

He got up early the next morning and built an altar at the foot of the mountain ... Then he sent young Israelite men, and they offered burnt offerings and sacrificed young bulls as fellow-ship offerings to the Lord. Moses took half of the blood and put it in bowls, and the other half he sprinkled on the altar. Then he took the Book of the Covenant and read it to the people. They responded, "We will do everything the Lord has said; we will obey."

Moses then took the blood, sprinkled it on the people and said, "This is the blood of the covenant that the Lord has made with you in accordance with all these words" (Exodus 19:3-6; 24:3-8).

As the book of Exodus opens, God's people are living in Egypt as slaves. They came there to escape famine in Canaan and they enjoyed the life God provided for them through Joseph. But after Joseph died, a new government came to power and things changed. Pharaoh viewed the growing numbers of the Children of Israel as a threat to his power. In response, he forced them into bitter slavery. Their experience was so bad that the very word "Egypt" came to symbolize slavery and death.

But these were the people of God. He had made promises to them and slavery was not one of them. Pharaoh's claims over the Israelites challenged the authority and plan of God. In addition, the bitterness of slavery grieved the heart of God, who never stopped loving His people. How could He *not* respond to their cries?

In time God raised up Moses as their deliverer and, through a series of awesome displays of power, set them free from Pharaoh's hand. Then, when it seemed Pharaoh had them cornered, God delivered them again at the Red Sea and destroyed the Egyptian army. The people of God were free, with a future to claim and enjoy.

But what did it *mean* to be God's people? And how could they access God's promised future? The first step into that future brought them to Mt. Sinai. Moses went to the top of the Mount where God gave him the seminar, "Being God's People." As soon as the people heard Moses' report from the Mount they agreed, "We will do everything the Lord has said." They chose to serve the Lord, a choice in favor of the relationship.

But the people still had much to learn about being God's people, and they would have to reaffirm their initial "Yes" to God. So Moses returned to the Mount and God continued to spell out the holy life of His people, letting them know what it meant to belong to Him. Then He gave Moses the Ten Commandments, along with additional instructions about living and serving Him (see Exodus 19-24).

When Moses shared these instructions with the people, they once again had to choose. Who would be Lord? Some other god or the Lord God Almighty who had set them free?

God's way of leading the Children of Israel helps us to understand our relationship with Him. Sooner or later we discover a basic clash of wills—ours against God's. Perhaps God wants us to make a career move or a lifestyle adjustment. Or, maybe we struggle with His call to be in the Word, spend more time in prayer, or meet the needs of someone near us. *Sooner or later, oneness with God means we will have to say what Jesus said, "Not as I will but as You will"* (Matthew 26:39, 42). Then the clash of wills ends and a deeper harmony comes to our love relationship with the Lord.

WHOM WILL YOU LOVE?

One of the teachers of the law came and heard them debating. Noticing that Jesus had given them a good answer, he asked Him, "Of all the commandments, which is the most important?"

"The most important one," answered Jesus, "is this: 'Hear, O Israel, the Lord our God, the Lord is one. Love the Lord your God with all your heart and with all your soul and with all your mind and with all your strength.' The second is this: 'Love your neighbor as yourself.' There is no commandment greater than these" (Mark 12:28-31).

Some people turn their love relationship with the Lord into something somber. Saying, "Not my will but Yours, O God," makes them deadly serious. It's easy to see how this can happen. After all, our partner in this relationship is perfect; His expectations are higher than we can ever see ourselves reaching. If we focus on all those expectations and then evaluate our performance honestly, we might never smile again! Worse still, we could easily forget we are in a love relationship with God. We could be like the fellow who thought reading and trying to practice rules from a marriage manual would make him a good husband.

Jesus never lost sight of the main point: we are called into an exclusive love relationship with God. As in any truly loving relationship, our primary concern is to deepen our love for God. Obedience should always grow out of love for God. Indeed, our obedience and our service to God are ways of saying, "I love You."

For example, God commands us to pray, worship, and witness. Our obedience to God demands that we do these things. But, in our praying we're consulting our Beloved and whispering our love to Him. In our worship we're setting aside time from a busy schedule to focus exclusively on Him, because He and our relationship with Him are worth it. In our witness we're sharing with others the love of our lives. Even when we're not consciously obeying, just keeping in mind that God is always with us is a way to share *everything* with our Life Partner. Obeying and serving God is how we tell Him, "I love You!"

Unfortunately, people in Jesus' day had a hard time grasping this point. During His ministry He had to contend with religious leaders who forgot that being God's people was a love relationship. For many, their religious life resembled a marriage where the partners no longer deeply loved each other but still went through the motions, creating an unconvincing impression of marital union. Thus, when they asked Jesus about the greatest commandment, they expected Him to analyze the various commands, rank them in priority, and discuss their possible ramifications. But Jesus refused to focus His attention on "going through the motions."

Instead, He insisted that a relationship with God must come from the heart. He called people to fan the flame of their devotion for God into a blazing and consuming fire. When asked about the greatest command, He recalled an ancient Jewish affirmation of faith: "Hear, O Israel, the Lord our God, the Lord is one" (Mark 12:29). Since there is but *one* God, *He* merits a singular, exclusive love. Therefore, we must love Him above and before we love anything or anyone else. Our deep love for God makes every other love seem lukewarm by comparison. In fact, love that is worthy of God will become passionate and fiery, consuming us, body, mind, spirit, soul. Every ounce of who we are will throb for God. And because we love Him, we will love other people, as God does. Time, energy, money, home, family, and everything else will become means of expressing this affection.

As we choose to serve God above all, our service will become "love in action." Jesus leads us not to focus on rules but on love. *The question is, "Who or what will claim our love in an exclusive sense?"* Self, other people, things, or God? Do our appointment book, social calendar, and checkbook suggest that we love God first? In the absence of passionate love for God, the most perfect conformity to all the rules will count for nothing. If we choose to love God fully and passionately, we will want to please Him, as all passionate lovers do their beloved. Keeping appropriate rules of conduct will never be an issue.

WHOSE WILL YOU BE?

> Therefore, I urge you, brothers, in view of God's mercy, to offer your bodies as living sacrifices, holy and pleasing to God—this is your spiritual act of worship. Do not conform any longer to the pattern of this world, but be transformed by the renewing of your mind. Then you will be able to test and approve what God's will is—His good, pleasing, and perfect will (Romans 12:1-2).

We serve God because we love Him and because we belong to Him. In love we have given ourselves to Him—that's what our initial commitment meant. But as soon as we are His, we become aware of competing interests. Surrounded by people and things claiming attention, time, and energy, we discover that some of those competing interests attract us. When this happens we must choose whose we will be.

In writing to Christians in Rome, Paul refers to altars and living sacrifices. Such imagery seems far removed from our contemporary culture. Yet, we too have altars on which we make sacrifices. For example, television, sports arenas, computers, homes, vacation spots, and workplaces—all qualify as modern altars. They represent pursuits to which we sacrifice, devote, or offer our possessions and ourselves. Some people lay their very lives on such altars, trying to find meaning and fulfillment.

Paul reminds us of "the mercy of God." In His mercy, God did not reject us when we rejected Him. Instead, He sent Jesus to show us His love. Through His sacrifice we have received a new life in right relationship with Him. God set us free from the power of sin and gave us His Spirit to empower a life pleasing to Him. And God promises He will never forsake us, but will bring us to a glory and triumph we now can only imagine (see Romans 1-11). How good God is to us!

Now, Paul says, make sure you are entirely His. Let there be no holding back, but give your whole self to God. That's the sacrifice you will want to offer—not a dead, but a living sacrifice. Put all you are and have at His disposal, all your abilities, potential, strengths, and weaknesses. Let Him work with you, with all of you.

Paul contends that anyone who truly understands God's mercy, and begins a love relationship with God, will want to go "all the way." No halfway measures or halfhearted commitments make sense. *Only our utter abandonment of all to God will do.*

In fact, that's the only way the relationship can work. Placing less than our all on the altar will lead us to confusion and uncertainty. We will not know God well enough to understand His ways and continue to please Him. Likewise, anything short of the total presentation of our lives to God will tempt us to conformity to whatever happens around us. We will not know God deeply enough to please Him consistently.

Can you imagine a marriage where one partner says to another, "I'll give you one day out of the week?" How absurd. But how about a marriage where one partner says, "I'm going to give you every day *but* one. On that day I'm on my own." Not even that would do. Partners who love one another hold nothing back. They give it all.

ONENESS WITH GOD

Once God forgives us and claims us as His own, we begin a wonderful love relationship. But when the glory and glow of "the honeymoon" fade, there's a life to live. We want to realize the full potential of the relationship, and only complete oneness and full intimacy with God will prove satisfying.

But intimacy requires that we continually deepen our relationship with God. He leads, we follow, and along the way we learn what our love for God means. These three passages we have considered help us to see how God works in our lives. As we understand how to please Him and identify the competing interests that attract us, we will want to choose God's will over our own. We will affirm our love for God above all else. And, we will settle for nothing short of being entirely His. *Giving ourselves to be entirely His leads to oneness with God.*

On August 16, 1975 I couldn't have loved Lavone more. We were as committed to each other as we knew how to be at the time. But we didn't want a mere "Kodak moment" for the scrapbook to show our friends the lovely wedding we had. We wanted oneness. We insisted on nothing less than all our love could promise.

So, when I learned who and how I was, and what I needed to do for our relationship to be all it could be, I began to do it. I truly loved this woman and desired a full return on her love for me. And, along the way, our relationship deepened. Our surrender to each other now is more full and complete than it was twenty years ago. It's not a perfect marriage and we haven't ironed out all the communication issues to our complete satisfaction. To be sure, I'm not beyond the possibility of hurting her. But we have a depth and quality of relationship, a kind of yieldedness, and a level of knowing each other, that convinces us we are one.

Our love relationship with God through Jesus travels a similar path. When God forgives us, we begin a special and holy relationship with Him. Just as He gave His all for us, so we give our all in return. But, as in any relationship, the potential for complete oneness and harmony must develop. As we choose God, His will, His love, and His way above all, He brings us into deep oneness with Himself. With Jesus we delight to do God's will (John 4:34; 5:30). And with Paul we can say, "For to me to live is Christ" (Philippians 1:21).

PART THREE

ON THE WAY OF HOLINESS

What does holiness look like?
And, are there "steps" to holiness?
When we ask about steps to anything,
we raise a modern question. Within
our culture we routinely ask about the
mechanics of process or endeavor. We want
a checklist that, if followed, will "get us there."

Relationships, however, don't work
that way. Whether with a friend,
a spouse, or God, there are no steps
to ascend or master, because relationships
are a rhythm of initiative and response
and require continuing openness.
In our relationship with God,

He makes the first move and we respond.
God then draws us to Himself and
leads us, and we continue to respond.

Our relationship with God works according
to this rhythm, as all relationships do.
God leads (initiative) and we follow
(response). As we walk with God
our initial forgiveness and our later
deepening oneness with God provide two
important landmarks on the way of holiness.
But these landmarks are not the whole journey.
From start to finish the journey envisions
ever-deepening companionship with the Holy One,
and we must always keep that vision before us.

Jesus shows us the holy life in action and
makes it possible for us to walk with Him,
the Holy One, on the way of holiness.
For, indeed, to be holy is to be like Jesus.
To walk on the way of holiness is to walk
with Jesus. In this sense, we can rightly
think about the steps on the way of holiness.
They are the daily steps we take
in following Jesus faithfully and fully.

CHAPTER SIX

Embracing the Cross

When we begin to follow Jesus, we start to walk in a different or *holy* way. We commence a journey toward Christlikeness, for, as we've seen, to be holy is to be like Jesus.

Do you protest even the thought of being like Jesus? You know yourself too well—how you think, speak, and react when the kids try your patience, the pressure mounts at work, or a hundred other common aggravations arise. These real-life experiences suggest to you that you can never really be like Him.

Yet, the New Testament teaches that you can. That was exactly what Jesus intended when He first called people to follow Him. In the gospels, once the first disciples responded to Jesus' call, it wasn't long before they were doing the very things Jesus did. He sent them out to preach the same message He preached, of repentance and the coming kingdom of God. He also empowered them for ministries of healing and casting out demons (see Matthew 10; Mark 6:6-13; Luke 9:1-6; 10:1-17). Certainly what Jesus expected them to do reveals His desire for them to be like Him.

Who can read the "Sermon on the Mount" (Matthew 5-7) and not see the character of Jesus shining through? If we live according to the Sermon, we're living like Jesus. And certainly that is what Jesus wants—for us to be like Him and live the way He did. Later, He called His disciples to make other disciples, among all peoples and in all places, who would learn and live according to His teachings (Matthew 28:16-20). In other words, Jesus came, lived, died, and rose again so that the world would be filled with people who are like Him.

To make all this possible, He promised to send the Holy Spirit whose presence in our lives makes Jesus shine through. The church described in the Book of Acts amazed the world because its members lived and acted like Jesus. Their opponents couldn't explain it except to note that they had been with Jesus (Acts 4:13).

The Apostle Paul affirms the same goal for all believers. He tells the church in Rome that God is at work in all the circumstances of their lives to accomplish what is good. And the ultimate good is to be like Jesus (Romans 8:28-29). To the Corinthians, who hardly qualified as the perfect church, Paul describes the Christian life as a glorious process of becoming more and more like Jesus, "We, who with unveiled faces all reflect the Lord's glory, are being transformed into His likeness with ever-increasing glory, which comes from the Lord, who is the Spirit" (2 Corinthians 3:18). And Paul prays for the Ephesian church, that they will be filled with all the fullness of God (Ephesians 3:19).

Throughout the New Testament, God calls us not only to admire Jesus' likeness, but to bear His likeness. Now, if God *calls* us to be like Jesus, don't you suppose we can be like Him?

What sort of a father would ask the impossible of his children? Not a very good one. As Jesus once said, we human fathers who could never win a Pulitzer Prize for goodness still know how to give good things to our children. How much more will our Heavenly Father give good things to His children (Matthew 7:11)? We may safely conclude that if God calls us to the great good of being and living like Jesus, it is possible. We should expect to become like Jesus, to be holy, as we walk with Him.

But how? I believe we find the answer in the story of Jesus. More precisely, the key to being like Jesus is His cross. Actually, the key to *Jesus* being like Jesus is the cross! Take away the cross and the story of Jesus hardly qualifies as "good news." If you delete Jesus' death on the cross, His story becomes the account of a storyteller, moral instructor, prophet, healer, and miracle worker. Impressive but not life-changing.

But the claim of the Bible is this: Jesus' story offers more than a string of good examples—it offers very good news! He came to show us our Father God who is wise, good, and eager to help us. Jesus helps us by connecting us to our Father God, by securing us in a loving relationship that will make us like our Father, as we see Him in Jesus, His Son. The help Jesus offers will make us holy.

At the heart of Jesus' work stands the cross. One day Jesus asked His disciples who the crowds thought He was. They gave a multiple-choice answer: some said He was John the Baptist returned from the dead, others said Elijah, and still others said Jeremiah or another of the prophets. But then Jesus put the question to them, "Who do *you* say I am?" Peter gave the correct answer— Jesus is the Son of God and the Messiah, the long-awaited King, who has come to help us and bring God's kingdom to us.

At that point, Peter and the others didn't understand what their correct answer would mean. But Jesus wasted no time in telling them. In effect, He said, "In order to help you to make God's kingdom a reality and give you the life and future God desires for you, *I must embrace the cross,* and so must you" (see Luke 9:18-25).

Here is the key to being like Jesus and being holy: embracing the cross. Let me describe three ways we need to embrace the cross as we follow Jesus on the way of holy living.

WE EMBRACE THE CROSS AS THE MEASURE OF GOD'S LOVE

How do we know when it's love—real, deep love coming our way? Especially when the Lover is God? God's answer to the question is the cross of Jesus.

> This is how God showed His love among us: He sent His One and only Son into the world that we might live through Him. This is love: not that we loved God, but that He loved us and sent His Son as an atoning sacrifice for our sins (1 John 4:9-12).

The phrase "as an atoning sacrifice" refers to Jesus' death on the cross. What does it do to you to realize that God gave His Son to die for you? And that the Father and Son collaborated in a costly act of love for *your* sake!? Has it become so familiar that it no longer moves you? The Apostle Paul marveled over this fact.

> You see, at just the right time, when we were still powerless, Christ died for the ungodly. Very rarely will anyone die for a righteous man, though for a good man someone might possibly dare to die. But God demonstrates His own love for us in this: While we were still sinners, Christ died for us (Romans 5:6-8).

I was privileged to attend the large clergy conference sponsored by the Promise Keepers organization in
February of 1996 in Atlanta, Georgia. A major theme of
the conference was racial harmony, and one speaker
told about an African-American marine who served on
the United Nations peace-keeping mission in Lebanon.
This marine, Jack, was on patrol one day with several
others in his platoon, including his best buddy, who
happened to be white. Toward the end of their patrol
duty someone tossed a hand grenade into the middle of
the platoon. Without thinking, Jack yelled, "Grenade!"
and shoved his buddy out of the way as he dove onto
the ground to smother the explosion. Jack had saved his
friend and the others by dying for them!

What a remarkable story. You can imagine how
those who were "saved" felt. The thought of this heroic,
sacrificial act must still overwhelm them with gratitude.
It's remarkable because it doesn't happen every day. But,
when it does happen, it's almost always a case of someone dying for *friends*. Few ever die for *enemies*, for those
who hate or mistreat them.

How different God is. How holy. While we were at
odds with God—yes, enemies—before we could ever respond, Jesus, knowing full well our worst defiance against
God, died for us. The Righteous for the unrighteous, the
Good for the evil, Jesus for you and me!

The cross shows us there is nothing God would
not do to fulfill His good plans for our lives. "He who
did not spare His own Son, but gave Him up for us all—
how will He not also, along with Him, graciously give us
all things?" (Romans 8:32). Therefore, if God calls us to
be like His Son Jesus, He will see that it happens!

We must embrace the cross as the sign of God's
deep love for us that opens before us all the possibilities

of His plan. His love becomes the basis on which we love Him and others. John reminds his Christian readers about Jesus' atoning sacrifice, "Dear friends, since God so loved us, we also ought to love one another" (1 John 4:11). And Peter agrees. Out of God's love and mercy He gives us new birth to a living hope and to a love for Jesus (see 1 Peter 1:3-9). On that basis, Peter urges his believing readers, "Love one another deeply from the heart. For you have been born again" (1 Peter 1:22-23).

In the cross we see the most impressive display of God's love for us. When that love flows into our hearts, it motivates us to let our lives be channels through which His love can flow. And, we will know that indeed it is *His* love because it will flow not only to the friend, but also to the enemy!

> Bless those who persecute you; bless and do not curse. ... Do not repay anyone evil for evil. ... If your enemy is hungry, feed him; if he is thirsty, give him something to drink. ... Do not be overcome by evil, but overcome evil with good (Romans 12:14-21).

Who can live this way? Only God *and* His godly or *holy* people. Only those who are like Jesus. The key to experiencing and sharing this deep, godly love is the cross of Jesus. By embracing it, we move into the way of Christlikeness or holiness.

WE EMBRACE THE CROSS AS THE WAY OF FORGIVENESS

How wonderful to know we are forgiven! Some time ago, one of our three daughters came home from school and was unusually quiet. Obviously, something was wrong. When her mom asked about her day, she began to cry. In class that day the students took a quiz, exchanged papers with a neighbor, and corrected them. Before handing hers in, on an impulse our daughter had changed a wrong answer to make it right. She knew better and as the day wore on she felt worse and worse. By suppertime it had become unbearable. "It feels so bad," she sobbed.

Immediately, Lavone scooped her up, held her gently, and explained, "Jesus is talking to you. You've done something wrong, and the only thing that will make it better is to ask Jesus to forgive you." Which she promptly did. Later that evening she exclaimed, "Mommy, I feel all new inside!"

When we do something wrong, consequences generally follow. What happens in a little girl's tender heart should happen in all of us. Wrongdoing *should* make us feel bad. That's the way God made us.

But the culture around us pretends that we can get away with it, that there will be no consequences. The world of television and cinema champions this view. Express your rage or your lust however you please, with hardly a consequence. When people drop like flies in the spray of a machine gun, how often do we see the brokenhearted families who may never heal from the wounds? The next time you watch a flirtation lead to attraction and then adultery, ask yourself about the spouses and kids at home. Where are they and what will they do when the truth hits home? When did you last see portrayed the sexual emptiness and dysfunction (something well documented in clinical studies) caused by allowing lust to run one's life? The media may claim that they are reflecting life in the real world, but truth without consequences always fails a "reality check."

When we embrace the cross of Jesus, we're admitting what the world denies—there *is* a price to pay and there *are* consequences. We suffer brokenness in our relationships with God, others, and ourselves because we are not right. We are wrong.

Jesus hung on the cross as a consequence of our sin. In His dying He assumes the eternal consequences. Embracing the cross means we accept this fact about ourselves, owning up to who we are and how we've lived. We claim no merit in God's presence and can do nothing to make up for our sin. In our brokenness and emptiness, we can only appeal to God to do something about it. By embracing and clinging to the cross, we accept Jesus' death for us as God's offer of forgiveness and pardon.

When we receive God's forgiveness, we change. We have a new relationship with God, the Creator and eternal Lord. We are okay with Him. And if we're okay with the Creator God, then we're okay period! If He can forgive us, we can forgive ourselves. We can stop beating ourselves up over what should or could have been. Instead, God can begin to build us up and shape us into what we should and can be.

God's forgiveness through Jesus' cross becomes the basis for an entirely new identity. Here we find the source of a proper, healthy view of ourselves as persons. Also, we find a new foundation for relating to other people in our lives.

Indeed, if God can forgive *us*, we can forgive others. Their sins against us cannot be excused, any more than our sins can be. But neither can they deal with their sins any better than we could handle ours. Only God can deal with sin and its consequences. And, if God can do that for *us*, He can do it for others. When we embrace the cross, we will want God to have His way with *all* sin and wrong. We trust God to do what only He can do. Just as we have sighed in relief and cried in praise because God has forgiven us and made us right, so we wait to see how God will work in the lives of those who have wronged us. Embracing the cross means delighting in our own forgiveness, *and* forgiving others in hope that they will one day share the same delight.

Forgiving others does not come naturally, especially if they have really hurt us. In chapter 2 I mentioned the Jansen family whose little girl was killed by a gang-related drive-by shooting. This family, quite naturally, wanted blood! I'm writing this chapter just after Timothy McVeigh's trial for bombing the Federal Building in Oklahoma City in April of 1995. Before the jury found McVeigh guilty and imposed the death sentence, one of the victims' relatives told a reporter it took two weeks for the rescue crews to find his wife's body. For fourteen days this man endured anxious suffering only to confirm his worst fears. What did this man want? "Ideally," he told the reporter, "McVeigh should be killed so that *his* loved ones can feel the same sort of pain." This suffering man shows us clearly the "normal" human response to painful offense—anything but forgiveness!

But people who embrace the cross are moving beyond "normal" human responses to something different. God has so overwhelmed them with His forgiveness and has launched them in such a different direction, that their responses are becoming holy, like Jesus.

We have all seen the unforgettable photo that made Pham Thi Kim Phuc famous. In June of 1972 an American bomber had just dropped a napalm bomb on her South Vietnamese village. The picture shows the horrible consequences: young Kim running, in the center of the road, naked, with body aflame, excruciating pain on her face.

Kim suffered third degree burns over much of her body that day. It took years to heal, and many surgical procedures. In the early years of the healing process, simply to change the bandages caused such pain that Kim passed out. We can only imagine how deep the emotional wounds were, the bitterness and anger that raged inside her, and the "natural" hatred she would have for Americans.

But there's another picture you may not have seen. It shows Kim, now a beautiful young adult, laying a wreath on the Vietnam War Memorial in Washington D.C.! After that photo session, she told reporters:

> I have suffered a lot from both physical and emo-
> tional pain. Sometimes I thought I could not live,
> but God saved my life and gave me faith and
> hope. ... Even if I could talk face to face with the
> pilot who dropped the bomb, I could tell him
> we cannot change history, but we should try to
> do good things for the present and for the future
> to promote peace.

In the audience that day was John Plummer, not the pilot but one partly responsible for bombing Kim's village. Later they met and a wonderful reconciliation occurred.[1]

What a strange, unnatural, holy response! Several years before this incident, Kim met Jesus. Through the cross God forgave her, cleansed away the bitterness of past hurts, and healed her on the inside. Having embraced the cross, Kim now walks on the way of forgiveness. She does the holy thing of sharing forgiveness with others. It's what Jesus does and what we can do as *we* embrace the cross.

Several months ago I saw a car with a personalized license plate. It read "IAM4GVN." I saw it and thought, "Yes! That is something to celebrate and to share." Embracing the cross makes it possible.

WE EMBRACE THE CROSS AS THE WAY TO FREEDOM

By nature we are self-centered creatures. We want what we want when we want it. If it's good for *us*, it's good! Certainly, we are more subtle and sophisticated than these blunt assertions suggest, but at the root of all that is not right with us is an obsessive, slavish concern for self. Spot a marriage in trouble, a shady business deal, a strained friendship, an unjust social system, a war, or a starving people; if we look closely we'll see a slavish concern for self.

It is impossible to have a balanced home, a close friendship, a deep satisfaction about life when we are constantly worried about ourselves. Jesus invites us to embrace the cross. "If anyone would come after Me, he must deny himself and take up his cross daily and follow Me" (Luke 9:23). Follow Him where? To the place of execution. We know Jesus was saying precisely this because in the next breath He explained, "For whoever wants to save his life will lose it, but whoever loses his life for Me will save it" (Luke 9:24).

The cross signals God's offer to deliver us from self-centered living. The Apostle Paul takes up Jesus' invitation to follow in terms of cross-bearing and ex- plains how it works. Accepting Jesus' invitation to fol- low Him to the place of death on the cross spells death to our "old self" or our old way of life. So much so that Paul can say, "I have been crucified with Christ and I no longer live, but Christ lives in me. The life I live in the body, I live by faith in the Son of God, who loved me and gave Himself for me" (Galatians 2:20).

When we begin to follow Jesus and embrace the cross, we die to a way of life dominated by selfishness so that we may live in a new way. In shouldering the cross, followers of Jesus are *free* to live like Jesus. Again Paul explains:

> Don't you know that all of us who were baptized into Christ Jesus were baptized into His death? We were therefore buried with Him through baptism into death in order that, just as Christ was raised from the dead ... we too may live a new life. ... For we know that our old self was crucified with Him so that the body of sin might be rendered powerless, so that we should no longer be slaves to sin—because anyone who has died has been freed from sin (Romans 6:3-7).

But what should we do with our new freedom? Paul says we must embrace the cross, just as Jesus did, "Count yourself dead to sin but alive to God in Christ Jesus. Therefore, do not let sin reign in your mortal body so that you obey its evil desires. Do not offer the parts of your body to sin" (Romans 6:11-13).

Before we first embraced the cross, we had no choice but to live for self, to do what human beings naturally do. This leads to all sorts of sin and the brokenness we know so well. But once we embrace the cross we are free for another way of life. We can make freedom from sinful selfishness the new norm for our lives. We can be like Jesus, free to bear the fruit of righteousness and holiness (see Romans 6:15-22).

Elsewhere Paul is more specific about what it means to put to death the old way of life.

Put to death, therefore, whatever belongs to your
earthly nature: sexual immorality, impurity, lust,
evil desires, and greed, which is idolatry. ... Now
you must rid yourselves of all such things as these:
anger, rage, malice, slander, and filthy language
from your lips (Colossians 3:5-8).

As we bring these qualities of the old life to their
death on the cross, we find a wonderful freedom to live
the new life.

Therefore, as God's chosen people, holy and
dearly loved, clothe yourselves with compassion,
kindness, humility, gentleness and patience. Bear
with each other and forgive whatever grievances
you may have against one another. Forgive as
the Lord forgave you. And over all these virtues
put on love, which binds them all together in
perfect unity (Colossians 3:12-14).

One summer several years ago, I fell desperately
ill with the worst flu I'd ever had. At first, I struggled to
keep going, but finally the illness disabled me. I lay flat
in bed, so nauseated that even turning from side to side
was unthinkable. Eventually, dehydration set in. Only
ignorance and maybe a bit of stubbornness kept me from
fearing for my life.

During these weeks of illness, all sorts of necessary
activities begged for my attention. I really wanted to rejoin
the living, but what I truly needed most was to get well!

As long as that bug had its way with me, I couldn't
even think about living the good life. My doctor offered
just what I needed, a prescription. He told me to take
it—not just until I started to feel better, but until there
was none left to take. The medicine had to be embraced
until it was completely consumed. If I stopped taking it

when I was well enough to resume minimal activity, the bug would make a comeback and I would have a setback. But if I took all my medicine, I would soon be free to resume a healthy life.

In a somewhat similar way, when we first embrace the cross to follow Jesus, He frees us from a life centered on self. As Paul put it, we bury the person we used to be and new life surges through us. But we must take all our medicine, the *whole dose.* We must continue to embrace the cross as the remedy God offers for the selfish and sinful life we would otherwise live.

Of course, my illustration isn't perfect. After I took all of my medicine and recovered, my life went on without medication. But as Christians, we never get beyond our need for the cross. If we stop embracing it, imagining that we no longer need the power of Jesus' cross in our lives, and begin to depend on ourselves, we will revert to our former selves. We will neither love as God loves, nor forgive as He forgives. Unless we continue to embrace the cross, we will not be free to live as Jesus would live.

HOW DO WE EMBRACE THE CROSS?

Jesus calls us to embrace the cross as He did. That's the only way we will understand how much He loves us and how much we may love Him and others. That's also the only way we may receive the wonderful gift of forgiveness from God and share it with others. Only in the cross can we find freedom from sin and selfishness that make a Christlike life impossible. Whenever selfishness stands in the way of loving and forgiving the way God does, Jesus invites us to embrace the cross. Nail the sin to the cross and leave it there, so that you can walk on in freedom.

Years ago, I was moving several heavy boxes from one part of our home to another. As always in those days my little girl was there to "help." "Daddy," she said, "*I* can do that. Let *me* carry it! Okay?" I said, "Okay!" It was obvious to me that she couldn't really do it, even though she really wanted to. So I watched with interest to see what would happen. She bent over, grabbed hold of a box, and quickly realized it was much heavier than she thought. Then, just as quickly, she looked up into my eyes and said, "Daddy, will you help me? Can we do it together?"

Who really did it? Since I supplied the strength, you might say I did. Yet, in a very real sense, she did too. She placed her will and desire—her all—in my hands as I lifted.

That's how *we* embrace the cross. Once we decide to follow Jesus, He gives us His Spirit. And from that moment on, the Holy Spirit works within our lives. He shows us the cross for what it is, He reveals our need for freedom to live as Jesus would live, and He empowers us to pick it up. We may look to the Spirit and ask, "Will You help me? Can we do it together?" As we surrender our will and desire to Him, we and He will do it together. And *He* will make us holy, like Jesus.

CHAPTER SEVEN

Living with Sacrifice

D uring the summer of 1996 thousands of athletes, and hundreds of thousands of others, gathered in Atlanta for the Summer Olympic Games. What a grand event, filled with drama, deep disappointment, and exhilarating delight. For those few weeks all sorts of activity and competition went on with a view to standing in the winner's spotlight, wearing a medal around the neck, cradling a bouquet of roses, and listening to the familiar sounds of the national anthem.

Those who enjoy their moment in the winner's circle are experts at delayed gratification. For years they have worked and trained, often overcoming enormous obstacles, all for a moment of ecstatic satisfaction. It is not uncommon to see tears stream down a winner's cheeks in the sheer joy and glory of the moment. These are people who have "gutted it out," and have gotten beyond the grind to the glory.

We have seen that the holy life means being like Jesus, following Him so closely that as we walk in His footsteps *we* become like *Him*. We've also seen that the key to being like Jesus is embracing the cross. As we do this, we experience God's deep love for us, we receive and reflect God's forgiveness, and we walk in freedom, empowered to center our lives on God and others. But *then* what? Having embraced the cross, can't we get past it as we anticipate glory?

FOLLOWERS OF JESUS NEVER GET BEYOND THE CROSS

The cross is not a necessary evil so that we can move quickly to the glory of a "resurrection life." Jesus didn't understand the cross in such terms. In fact, He offered cross-bearing as the model for an *entire life* of discipleship. "You must take up your cross *daily*" (Luke 9:23, emphasis added). Since we never get beyond following Jesus, we will never get beyond carrying or bearing the cross.

There can be no doubt that the first followers of Jesus understood Him in just this way. Chief among them was the Apostle Paul, who constantly described daily Christian living in terms of the cross of Jesus. We've already recalled what he told the Galatians, "I have been crucified with Christ and I no longer live, but Christ lives in me" (Galatians 2:20). The cross was foundational for Paul and also the primary material he used to build his life:

> Whatever was to my profit I now consider loss for the sake of Christ. What is more, I consider everything a loss compared to the surpassing greatness of knowing Christ Jesus my Lord, for whose sake I have lost all things. I consider them rubbish, that I may gain Christ and be found in Him, not having a righteousness of my own that comes from the law, but that which is through faith in Christ—the righteousness that comes from God and is by faith. I want to know Christ and the power of His resurrection and the fellowship of sharing in His sufferings, becoming like Him in

His death, and so, somehow, to attain to the resurrection from the dead (Philippians 3:7-11).

Paul looked forward to being in the winner's circle with Christ and sharing in the glory of the resurrection. But on the way to the winner's circle, he saw his life in terms of cross-bearing—sharing in Christ's sufferings and being like Him in His death.

He said the same thing to the Corinthians, "We always carry around in our body the death of Jesus, so that the life of Jesus may also be revealed in our body. For we who are alive are always being given over to death for Jesus' sake, so that His life may be revealed in our mortal body" (2 Corinthians 4:10-11). In order for Jesus' likeness to shine through, holy living requires cross-bearing. Paul never got beyond this.

But what about living in the power of the resurrection? Doesn't God call us to live by this power? Indeed. Remember what Paul told the church at Rome, "We were therefore buried with Him through baptism into death in order that, just as Christ was raised from the dead ..., we too may live a new life" (Romans 6:4). This new life of following Jesus faithfully brings us back full circle to the cross. God fills us with His Spirit and the power of the resurrection so that we may take up our cross *daily* and be like Jesus. That's what Paul meant when he told the Corinthians, "We have this treasure [the gospel and the life it gives us] in jars of clay [the frail, broken human person] to show that this all-surpassing power [*resurrection* power] is from God and not from us" (2 Corinthians 4:7, my explanatory comments). When people see Spirit-empowered cross-bearing, they can't help but notice that God is at work in our lives.

Other voices in the New Testament chime in with Paul's. The writer of Hebrews says, "So Jesus also suffered outside the city gate to make the people holy through His own blood. Let us, then, go to Him outside the camp, bearing the disgrace He bore" (Hebrews 13:12-13). As it was with Jesus, so it is with His followers—the whole of life can be summarized as "going to the cross!"

Similarly, Peter writes to slaves suffering under cruel masters, "If you suffer for doing good and you endure it, this is commendable before God. To this you were called, because Christ suffered for you, leaving you an example, that you should *follow* in His steps" (1 Peter 2:20-21, emphasis added). As followers of Jesus, walking with Him on the way of holiness, we never get beyond the cross. Therefore, holiness means sacrifice.

FOLLOWERS OF JESUS LIVE A LIFE OF SACRIFICE

What else could Jesus' call to take up the cross mean, if not sacrifice? But, that's not how we often think about following Jesus, is it? In the American culture, being a Christian is often promoted as a way to self fulfillment, emotional happiness, and material success. We hear Jesus' invitation to follow Him, and yet quickly forget the element of sacrifice. We hear, "Follow Jesus so that when you die you'll have the right answer that will admit you to heaven." Or, "Commit to Jesus' way of life and your depression, loneliness, emotional pain, physical illness, or stalled car will be all right."

But is it possible to follow Jesus without sacrifice? To take up the cross as Jesus did without at the same time foregoing some desirable things—whether possessions, experiences, freedoms, comforts, or conveniences? Taking up the cross, by its very nature, means sacrifice. And, to do it daily means a life of sacrifice. Jesus made this point with special force, in His call to rigorous discipleship (Luke 9:23-26). But He didn't leave the matter there, assuming that His disciples would know what that meant. Instead, He proceeded to Jerusalem, where cross-bearing would lead to His death. On the way to His appointment with the cross, He taught what cross-bearing means.

Most of Jesus' teaching on discipleship in Luke's gospel comes "on the way to the cross" and this teaching has "sacrifice" written all over it. The Good Samaritan's sacrifice meant time, energy, money, and bodily danger to help someone in need, even someone who hates your kind (10:25-37). For Martha, sacrifice involved setting aside social custom to give full attention to Jesus (10:38-42). The rich fool, who never had enough even though he had no needs, modeled a disdain for sacrifice that proved deadly. For him sacrifice would have meant holding things more loosely in order to get a firm grasp on God (12:16-21). For some households, sacrifice meant choosing Jesus over loved ones, and losing the benefits of family life (12:49-53).

Sacrifice for the host and guests at the banquet called for humility and a rejection of the self-seeking and status that others find perfectly acceptable (14:1-14). Sacrifice means counting the cost and going the whole way with Jesus, no matter how high the price (14:15-34). For religious insiders who enjoy the security and blessings of belonging to God, sacrifice requires a radical openness and gracious welcome toward "unworthies" whose former life offends cultured spirituality (15:1-32). For the rich, being right with God would lead to generous care of the poor (16:19-31), or simply giving everything away to be free to follow Jesus wholly (18:18-29).

Not every disciple will do all of these things. Not

everyone in Jesus' day, or in the life of the early church, assumed every form of sacrifice. But, as earnest followers of Jesus, all of them were well-acquainted with sacrifice. Those who seriously walked with Him lived, gave, and served in sacrificial ways. According to the New Testament, sacrifice is the norm for followers of Jesus.

Too often, we think of sacrifice as the exception rather than the norm. And, it's no wonder. Sacrifice is hard, and who likes hard? Invite people to sacrifice and you'd better prepare for loneliness! How many would become Christians these days if we insisted that the way of Christ is one of sacrifice?

These questions merit close attention. On the surface people may seem to prefer avoiding sacrifice at all costs. But, at a deeper level, most of us are highly attracted to sacrifice. Let me explain.

I love to hear gifted musicians—whether the great masters of classical music or the newer varieties of musical genius. Few gifted musicians were born with their expertise; most had to sacrifice to develop their talent and they continue to sacrifice in order to bless those who hear them. I find that sort of sacrifice incredibly attractive!

We live in a town that is crazy for basketball. Our high school boys team has made a habit of winning the state championship tournament each year. We are so accustomed to their "winning it all" that a second-place finish no longer merits a celebration. But none of those young basketball champions could enjoy such triumph without all kinds of sacrifice along the way. For most of them the sacrifices began in early elementary school!

You can't even grow a garden without some sacrifice of time and energy and money. Most communities find their beauty enhanced by the green thumbs of their citizens, but not without considerable care and labor.

Each spring we celebrate the graduation of high school and college students. But there could be no party without sacrifice. I think we all know deep down that the best things in life simply do not happen apart from sacrifice.

At some point, most of us have been not only attracted to sacrifice but deeply committed to it as essential to our lives. How could we have gotten our education or excelled in our work without sacrifice—our own and that of others? How could we raise our children and send them into the world as mature disciples of Jesus without making some sacrifices along the way? If we ever do anything well, it happens because we have made any number of sacrifices in order to learn, practice, and develop.

WHAT DO YOU WANT MOST?

My question to you is not, "Do you live a life of sacrifice?" Rather, I ask you, "What are your goals? What is your aim in life? What do you really, truly want? What is supremely important to you?" Trivial matters do not call for sacrifice. But important goals always require sacrifice. Therefore, we shouldn't be surprised if sharing in the kingdom of God and being like the Son of God mean sacrificial living.

But let's be clear: we're not called to sacrifice in order to be acceptable or right before God. We rely *only* on God's love offered to us in Jesus' death to give us new life. Only what God does *for* us makes us acceptable in His presence.

But God has no interest in making us mere trophies to His goodness. He aims to make us His people. He calls us to *be* like Jesus. That aim of God, when taken earnestly, always leads to sacrifice.

Jesus' followers become Olympic in their desires and efforts at following Him and pursuing His goals. With World Series earnestness they invest their time and energy in Jesus' name for His cause. Their calendars suggest radical commitment to following Jesus. With World Cup zeal they make their possessions available to bless others, to be used so others will know God's love and develop into Jesus-like people. When they do their taxes on their personal computers, the auditing function asks them about their contributions to the church and charities because they give so much. People who know them can hardly believe their openness and concern, their willingness to listen and share, and their eagerness to demonstrate Jesus' way of dealing with life.

Jesus' followers join the Apostle Paul in saying, "One thing I do: Forgetting what is behind and straining toward what is ahead, I press on toward the goal to win the prize for which God has called me heavenward in Christ Jesus" (Philippians 3:13-14). This straining, stretching, and pressing on conditions all they are, all they have, and all they do.

A friend of mine pastors a Mennonite church near our town. Recently, a man from Zaire, Africa, now the Democratic Republic of Congo, visited his church. This man had come to share recent happenings in Central African Mennonite Missions.

As they drove from the airport to the church, my friend asked his guest if he had ever heard of Larry Kauffman. Larry had gone as a missionary to Zaire from my friend's congregation more than forty years ago. He served there for just a short time, however, before dying in a drowning accident.

At the mention of Larry Kauffman's name, the African's face lit up as he said, "I didn't know Larry was from here! Yes, I knew him rather well!" Then, he went on to tell of the impact of this missionary's life and death among them.

Through the missionary's death, the church in Zaire came to understand that following Jesus meant willingness to go halfway around the world and, if necessary, to die. What blessing this missionary's life of sacrifice had brought to thousands in Zaire!

As I consider God's call to be like Jesus, I have a twofold reaction. First, from deep within me there is a yearning, a longing that cries out, "Yes!" This is what I truly desire—to be like Jesus and to make a difference in the world by following Him.

But my second response is a kind of nagging question, "What does this life of sacrifice mean for me?" It's not really a guilt trip, but a continuing quest to find answers to that question and shape my life accordingly. It's a question I ask in relation to my use of time, money, and energy. It's one by which I evaluate my comfortable life, family, and church. This unsettling question surfaces when I see what's going on elsewhere in the world and even in my own backyard.

It's a good question because through asking it, God's Spirit draws me closer to Jesus and to His likeness. This yearning to be like Jesus, whatever it may require, comes from the Lord. And, as with all God-given desires, the Spirit will work to make it so.

CHAPTER EIGHT

Accepting the Mantle of Servanthood

W hen we encounter a holy God, we soon find ourselves serving. We've seen the experience of Isaiah—once God met his need, he was ready to say, "Here am I. Send me" (Isaiah 6:8). Likewise, when Peter recognized Jesus as the Holy One, he was called to a different kind of fishing (Luke 5:10).

Jesus Himself models the sort of ministry to which holiness always leads. Paul reminded the Philippian church that the whole life of Jesus can be told in terms of humble, obedient service. He may have been citing a poem or hymn as he wrote:

> Your attitude should be the same as that of Christ Jesus: Who, being in very nature God, did not consider equality with God something to be grasped, but made Himself nothing, taking the very nature of a servant, being made in human likeness. And being found in appearance as a man, He humbled Himself and became obedient to death—even death on a cross! (Philippians 2:5-8)

In John's gospel we find a moving story of how Jesus modeled servanthood (John 13:1-17). On the night before the crucifixion, He rose from the supper table, where He was recognized by the disciples as Master-teacher and Lord, and began to act like the lowest slave. John explains, "Having loved His own who were in the world, He now showed them the full extent of His love" (John 13:1). Jesus demonstrated His love that evening by washing the disciples' feet; but eventually, "the full extent of His love" nailed Him to the cross. Students of the Bible often see a connection between these two acts: the footwashing expresses a common, everyday example of Jesus' uncommon, or holy, service that climaxed on the cross. Let's look more closely at what Jesus did.

THE SETTING

It's always helpful to know the circumstances in which a person acts. In this case, it was the season of Passover (John 13:1). These were days of high expectation, much like we have just before Christmas or Easter. Special activities and celebrations filled a family's calendar.

The Passover itself celebrated God's deliverance of His people from slavery and death in Egypt. Through Moses the Lord had repeatedly demanded His people's release from Egyptian bondage. Yet Pharaoh stubbornly refused, despite a series of plagues on his land and people. Finally, God's patience ran out and He determined to pass through the land in judgment so that every first-born person and animal would die. But there was one way to escape this judgment. The Lord told His people to take a year-old lamb without spot or blemish, slaughter it, and place some of its blood on the top and the sides of their doorways. When the messenger of death saw the blood, he would *pass over* their households. In the Passover feast, then, the people celebrated God's

gift of life instead of death, and freedom instead of slavery. Every year they rejoiced to know that God desires
His people to be free and truly alive. The story is recorded in Exodus 1-13.

Jesus' disciples were about to begin a new chapter of Passover observance. I wonder if they recalled
that day a few years earlier when John the Baptizer saw
Jesus and shouted, "Look, the Lamb of God, who takes
away the sin of the world!" (John 1:29). That was the
anticipation—that the Lamb of God would be sacrificed
to bring real life and freedom within reach!

WHAT JESUS KNEW

It's always helpful to know what people are thinking when they act. John tells us that Jesus was fully aware
of what lay ahead. What He did was deliberate and pur-
poseful.

Jesus realized His time was up, which is important for us to know in appreciating the story. Usually,
we don't know how much time we have. If we did,
what a difference it would make! If we knew we had
only today or this week, that knowledge would affect
what we said and did. Indeed, we would do and say
only the most important things. Wasting time would be
out of the question. So, let's watch Jesus. What He said
and did on this occasion are of utmost importance for
life and freedom!

Jesus also knew that one of His own disciples
would betray Him (see John 13:11). Frankly, I'm glad I
don't know everything! I'm content to stay in the dark,
not aware of all the disappointments and tragedies be-
forehand. I think it would be as much curse as blessing
to know such things in advance.

One of these dear friends—handpicked by Jesus,

now a confidant and partner in ministry—would betray Him. Despite the bright hopes and big plans Jesus had, the devil would have his way with Judas. How heart-breaking! What an emotional load that adds to the picture. Could it be that Jesus wanted to try one last time to show Judas His love, to convince him to take another course of action?

Jesus also knew that His Father had put all things under His power (John 13:3). Whatever happened next, Jesus would not be a victim. He would not be forced to do anything He didn't want to do. No compulsion or necessity drove Him, except one—to show the full extent of His love. He had been sent as the Lamb of God to die so that we might live and be free. But His mission in the world and His dying on the cross was lavish love, shocking in its extravagance. Just how shocking He was about to demonstrate.

WHAT JESUS DID

First, He interrupted the meal. The food was on the table and they'd all begun to eat, but Jesus got up from His place at the table. Remember, time was slipping away and permitted only the most important words and deeds. What Jesus was about to do was more important than celebrating the holiday, so important that essential and good activities must come to a halt. No doubt the interruption would make the event more memorable. But, even more, to disrupt the festivities in this way would send a clear signal: what Jesus was about to do ranked right up there with eating and sharing fellowship around the table. Here we have an essential of life for His followers.

Footwashing was a common way of showing respect to a guest, and ordinarily, a slave would perform this service. Jesus identified with the lowest of the low when He stripped to the waist, wrapped the towel around Himself, and took the basin to the first disciple, and began to wash His feet.

Be assured, He was breaking social protocol. People of His stature and status simply didn't do such things—they were deserving of service from others. Probably everyone around the table thought, "Somebody's gotta do something!" And, finally, Peter raised the right protest, "Jesus, this is too much!"

Jesus turned everything upside down by taking up the towel and basin. He wanted to show them, and us, that no one is unworthy of being served and no one is too important to serve. At least, that's the way it works in the new culture of God's kingdom. So, in effect, Jesus replied, "Among My people and in My Father's kingdom, this is exactly the kind of thing we do!" For those of us who follow *Him,* pride must not keep anyone from serving or being served. And love must move us to serve one another.

When Jesus finished washing their feet and returned to the table, He asked His disciples, "Do you understand what I have done?" I wonder if He saw glimmers of recognition, or just blank stares? Not waiting for an answer, He told them, "I'm the Teacher and Lord. Now let me show you the way, the *only* way. I've just given you an example of how My people relate to others. If *this* is what I do, *this* is what you should do" (my paraphrase of John 13:13-15).

DISCIPLES WHO PUT JESUS' LESSON INTO PRACTICE

■ In 1967 Doug Nichols was serving in India with Operation Mobilization, a Christian relief organization. Shortly after his term of service began, he came down with tuberculosis. Even worse, the only means of treatment open to him required several months in a TB sanitarium. So, there he was: sick and disappointed, among fellow patients and hospital staff whose language he did not know!

Since Doug was committed to sharing Christ wherever he was, he determined to serve the Lord in *that* place. As strength allowed, he gave out tracts telling about Jesus. He noted that the people received the leaflets with a smile, but then later threw them into the trash. What a sense of failure he felt.

Then one night things began to change. Doug awoke at 2 a.m. with a fit of coughing and wheezing. Just as he calmed down, he noticed an older and sicker man across the room trying to get out of bed. He would sit up, inch toward the edge and try to stand, only to fall back into bed, crying softly. The next morning Doug realized what the man was trying to do—simply go to the bathroom. Soon everyone knew about it, as the terrible stench of his accident quickly spread throughout the ward. Other patients, and even the staff, yelled at the man and abused him for the mess he had made.

The next night it was the same story. The man tried, but couldn't get up, and fell back into bed whimpering.

Doug will tell you he hates bad smells and really didn't want to get involved. Even so, he approached the man's bed, looked into his frightened eyes and gained silent permission to pick him up. He carried the man to the room where there was just a hole in the ground and held him up while he took care of himself. When Doug returned the man to his bed, the man said something he didn't understand and kissed him on the cheek.

The next morning another patient came over and

offered Doug a steaming cup of tea. Then he began to make motions until Doug realized he was asking for one of the gospel tracts. Throughout the day, others also came and asked for the little booklets about Jesus.

Later Doug learned that a number of people eventually decided to follow Jesus, but not because they found the tracts so persuasive. It was because Doug had followed the example of Jesus by taking that trip to the bathroom. Jesus said, "If *this* is what I do, *this* is what you should do!"[1]

■ I first met Don when we were both students in seminary. We became friends but drifted apart after graduation, eventually losing all contact. Then, fifteen years later, I saw him at a minister's conference. Don told me God had called him to be a church planter in the South. Remarkably, over the last several years he had seen one church begin, grow to about 250 regular attenders, and then spin off a daughter congregation. Then another and another. At the time of our meeting they were working on their fourth church plant.

One key strategy for letting folk in the community know they were followers of Jesus especially caught my attention. They organized teams of two or three to make themselves available to perform services no one else was likely to do. For example, armed with rubber gloves and cleaning supplies, they visited area restaurants, businesses, or recreation centers and asked if they could clean their bathrooms. And when they heard the inevitable question, "Why do you want to clean them?" they answered, "Because we are followers of Jesus!" Indeed, Jesus said, "If *this* is what I do, *this* is what you should do."

■ Kevin Miller, editor of *Leadership* magazine, tells about his father who passed away several years ago. Mr. Miller had been a vice-president at Harper &

Row Publishers, impressive in the outside world and also in the world he shared with his son. In one of Kevin's most vivid memories, his dad came into the room saying, "C'mon kid, let's go." "Where to?" Kevin asked. "Lucy's!"

Once a month Mr. Miller visited Lucy, a woman whose body had been twisted and pinned to a wheelchair by arthritis. During those visits he would pick her frail body up out of the chair, place her in the front seat of the car, fold the chair, put it in the trunk, and take her for a drive. Here was a VIP shuttling a shut-in. Yes, because Jesus said, "If *this* is what I do, *this* is what you should do."[2]

■ Every year during Advent we have an all-church "Caroling and Chili Event." We gather in the Fellowship Hall, organize into mini-choirs, and go caroling, especially visiting people who are homebound. Then, after making the rounds, we return to the church to enjoy some piping hot chili.

One year Lavone and I led a group to a care facility in town. Up and down the halls we roamed, serving the residents by bringing them a hearty dose of Christmas cheer. On one of our stops we were near the room of a lady who eagerly rolled her wheelchair to the door to see and hear us. As we sang "Joy to the World," out of the corner of my eye, I noticed a young lady in our group stooping down to help this dear woman recover the slipper she had lost in wheeling her chair to the hallway. Most of us didn't even notice the need, but this young lady did and then met it. By far, the most notable thing about our visit was not our singing, but this act of attentive care. Jesus said, "If *this* is what I do, *this* is what you should do."

WHAT JESUS WANTS TO DO

Jesus calls us to be servants as He was. Now, having called us, He wants to make it so! If you're like me, you are both attracted and repulsed by what Jesus wants us to do. On the one hand, what beautiful and moving stories can be told about people who serve the way Jesus did. The beauty of these stories, and the wonderful impact such service has on others, draws us toward Jesus-style service.

But, on the other hand, most of us are not greatly attracted to dusty feet, sick people, or dirty bathrooms. Nor do we automatically get excited about spending time and energy in such service, seeing as we have enough of our own work all the time.

And we're not so sure about being on the receiving end either. Do we really want other people washing our feet or otherwise stepping in to help us? Do we even want others to know when we have needs? We are both attracted and repulsed!

Well, there's good news and bad news. The bad news is that Jesus doesn't give us options at this point. He isn't offering a suggestion for us to consider. He told Peter, "Unless you let *Me* do this for *you*, you can't have anything to do with Me" (John 13:8, emphasis mine). Then He told all of them, "I have set you an example that you should do as I have done for you" (John 13:15). Followers of Jesus will routinely find themselves on both ends of "towel and basin" service.

But here's the good news: we don't become servants on our own. We may hear Jesus' call and may desire to say "Yes," but unless He first serves us, we will never be able to serve others as He did.

And, of course, Jesus is eager to serve us in this way. He has loved us "to the end." Remember the setting of the footwashing, just before Passover? Jesus is the Lamb of God, sacrificed to take away the sin of the world. His sacrifice makes us alive and free in the same way He was.

Jesus wants to free us to use our "powers," our abilities, resources, and energies to serve others. We don't have to be insecure and thus always grasping for control. Nor do we need to hang on tightly to what we have, for fear of losing it!

Jesus wants to free us to serve—even to be kind, considerate, and helpful toward the enemy. One pair of feet Jesus washed belonged to Judas!

Jesus wants to free us to develop servant eyes that see how we may be helpful, and servant hearts that will move us to help.

Jesus would also like to free us so that we can receive the service of others. He wants to make His followers into a community of mutual serving. And to accomplish His plan He desires to cleanse away the pride and self-consciousness that keeps us from serving others and from allowing others to serve us.

I suspect that most of us would much rather be on the serving end of things. Through the years, I've had several friends much wealthier than I. Do you think they ever let me pick up the check when we have lunch together? Not on your life! At least, not without a great deal of urging, and sometimes sneaking around, on my part. They mean well, and I deeply appreciate their generosity. But, as I've tried to explain on several occasions, it really would be a treat for me to entertain them. It feels good to give!

Who pays for lunch probably won't count for eternity, but the hesitancy to let other people serve us may have profound consequences. Think about the person facing a serious need—a suspicious shadow on the X ray requiring some diagnostic tests or exploratory surgery; a child making a poor choice, leaving parents grief-stricken; a work situation creating mile-high anxiety; a company's downsizing that threatens a family's security. In each of these situations and others like them, a refusal to be served hurts both those who would love to serve in Jesus' name and those who would be helped by receiving. A hesitancy to let others serve us robs Christians of an opportunity to show the church family and an unbelieving world what following Jesus really means. And that's what Jesus wants—to show the world His love through us as a community of *mutual serving*.

If this is what Jesus wants to do for us, then *how* does He do it? I'm sure that if Jesus could physically walk beside us in our daily lives, we wouldn't ask this question. In each situation, Jesus would show us the way. If His signals weren't clear, we could ask Him to clarify His will. But, of course, that's impossible. Jesus can't physically walk beside every one of us.

No, but He can do something even better (see John 16:7). He promised to send His disciples the Holy Spirit, to be a companion to them. Even more, He said the Spirit would be within His disciples to reveal and make clear the way of Jesus and then empower them to walk on that way.

So, how does Jesus do this work of cleansing and empowering that frees us to serve as He did? When we first began to follow Jesus, He kept his word and gave us His Spirit. In ways we cannot fully understand, much less explain, the Spirit "lives" within us.

In other words, it's an inside job! If we ask the Spirit to accomplish Jesus' plan in us and through us, we may be sure He will. And, by the way, He is the *Holy*

Spirit. As He cleanses us and empowers us to follow Jesus, He makes us servants and holy.

CHAPTER NINE

Accomplishing the Mission of Jesus

When I was a boy, "Mission Impossible" was a favorite TV program. Each episode began with Jim, played by Peter Graves, receiving a top-secret message via tape recorder, which was usually found in some obscure place. Sometimes simply locating the tape was nearly impossible! The actual missions varied, but all of them were of life and death importance and commanded the very best from the agents who accepted them. And, of course, *all* of them were "impossible."

In chapter 8 we saw that individual followers of Jesus, on the way of holiness, will inevitably take up the towel and basin as God's servants to others. In this chapter we will discover that God's servant-people are also on a mission *together* in the world, a mission that will strike some as incredible, even impossible.

We are, after all, followers of Jesus and He was on a mission, one that He announced shortly after He began His public life:

> Jesus returned to Galilee in the power of the Spirit, and news about Him spread through the whole

countryside. He taught in their synagogues, and everyone praised Him.

He went to Nazareth, where He had been brought up, and on the Sabbath day He went into the synagogue, as was His custom. And He stood up to read. The scroll of the prophet Isaiah was handed to Him. Unrolling it, He found the place where it is written: "The Spirit of the Lord is on Me, because He has anointed Me to preach good news to the poor. He has sent Me to proclaim freedom for the prisoners and recovery of sight for the blind, to release the oppressed, to proclaim the year of the Lord's favor" (Luke 4:14-19).

Jesus told the people that His ministry would fulfill these prophetic words. Following Jesus means accepting *His* mission as *our own.* We take our cue from the disciples on this point. Once they began to follow Jesus, it wasn't long before He sent them out on a mission.

He gave them power and authority to drive out all demons and to cure diseases, and He sent them out to preach the kingdom of God and to heal the sick ... So they set out and went from village to village preaching the gospel and healing people everywhere (Luke 9:1-2, 6).

Remarkably, these twelve disciples did exactly what Jesus had been doing. And, they did it so well that people began to wonder if resurrection powers hadn't been unleashed among them (see Luke 9:7-9). Jesus' mission was *their* mission.

But this mission assignment was not only for the twelve disciples. Jesus called *all* of His followers to join Him.

The Lord appointed seventy-two others and sent

them two by two ahead of Him to every town and place where He was about to go. He told them, "The harvest is plentiful, but the workers are few. Ask the Lord of the harvest, therefore, to send out workers into His harvest field. Go! I am sending you out like lambs among wolves (Luke 10:1-3).

Jesus told them to pray about the needs of the mission, and then He answered their prayers by sending *them*! Again, make no mistake, this was none other than Jesus' mission, as we can see from their report: "The seventy-two returned with joy and said, 'Lord, even the demons submit to us in Your name'" (Luke 10:17).

If any doubt remains, some of Jesus' last instructions to His disciples (and through them to us) confirm that we are on a mission as God's holy people. On Easter evening Jesus appeared to His fearful and confused followers to give them the gift of peace and to lay out the plans for their (and His) continuing mission.

He opened their minds so they could understand the Scriptures. He told them, "This is what is written: The Christ will suffer and rise from the dead on the third day, and repentance and forgiveness of sins will be preached in His name to all nations, beginning in Jerusalem. You are witnesses of these things. I am going to send you what My Father has promised; but stay in the city until you have been clothed with power from on high" (Luke 24:45-49).

The book of Acts continues the story as Jesus instructs the disciples to wait for the promised Holy Spirit. When the Spirit came in awesome power, the energized followers of Jesus moved out into the world to accomplish their mission.

THE MISSION

The holiness of Jesus' followers can perhaps be seen most clearly at the point of mission. Most other groups in the world exist for the sake of self—the individual self and the group's welfare. They keep the benefits of their members most in mind. But the people of God are different from other groups at this point. They have a mission from Jesus based on His teaching, "Whoever wants to save his life will lose it, but whoever loses his life for Me will save it" (Luke 9:24). So, Jesus' followers, made holy by His presence among them, live for the sake of God and others. As Archbishop William Temple once observed, "The church is the only cooperative society in the world which exists for the sake of its nonmembers."[1] *That* is the difference which expresses our mission as the holy people of God.

I've tried to imagine and implement what it means for the church truly to exist for others. No less than a complete change of attitude and orientation may be required in the whole church or within its various groups. Sociologists claim that most of us have from six to eight people near us whom we could influence for Jesus. What would happen if the small groups of our churches began to ask, "Who are these people close to us? What makes them tick? What are their needs and hurts? What would God like to do in their lives? How could we help God accomplish His will for them?" Then, suppose we not only asked such questions, but let them set the agenda for the church's programs and ministries. I think we'd be preparing ourselves for exciting days in mission!

By "mission" I don't necessarily mean going to Africa or South America. Nor do I refer to moving into an urban center to work in a soup kitchen. And, I don't mean becoming a pastor. Of course, "mission" *could*

mean any or all of these, and I would encourage serious followers of Jesus to consider such options!

Rather, I'm using "mission" to describe our orientation and perspective in life. Mission speaks to the sense
of purpose we have as we make our way through life
following Jesus. Mission refers to the destiny which is
rooted in our identity as people of God.

THE "ALIENS"

In First Peter we find special insight into our mission as holy people. To begin, Peter uses two interesting
phrases to describe Christian people. He calls them "visiting strangers" and "resident aliens." These terms have
been translated variously as "exiles," "aliens," and "strangers," to describe people who found themselves either
passing through foreign territory or temporarily living in
a foreign country. Almost always some calamity had
forced them from their homes to foreign soil—famine,
plague, or war. To be "strangers" or "aliens" meant they
didn't belong, even if they had settled down, built homes,
and found work. Since they lacked "native" or "citizen"
status, they were denied the rights and privileges that
others around them enjoyed. For that reason, they would
likely suffer at least mild forms of discrimination, if not
blatant persecution.

Peter uses these terms to describe the situation of
Christians in the world. God has made them a new and
different kind of people and for that reason they live the
life of "aliens" and "strangers" (see 1 Peter 1:1, 17; 2:11).
Christians do not trace their true roots to others in this
world, but to God. Because He has called His people to
be different or holy (see 1:14-16), they live as "aliens
and strangers."

Jesus had said of His followers that they were in

the world, but not of the world (John 17:11, 14). The Apostle Paul made the same point to his friends in Philippi. "But our citizenship is in heaven. And we eagerly await a Savior from there, the Lord Jesus Christ" (Philippians 3:20). Likewise, the writer of Hebrews celebrated the faithful of old as models for our life of faith:

> By faith Abraham, when called ... obeyed and went, even though he did not know where he was going. By faith he made his home in the promised land like a stranger in a foreign country. ...
>
> All these people were still living by faith when they died. They did not receive the things promised; they only saw them and welcomed them from a distance. And they admitted that they were aliens and strangers on earth (Hebrews 11:8-13).

Peter's imagery—identifying us as "aliens"—reminds us that belonging to God and to His kingdom affects everything about us, the work we do and, even more, how we do it; the people we associate with and those with whom we establish deep friendships; the one we marry and those we date before we marry; what we do with our time; how we spend our money; how and what we plan for the future. Belonging to God rather than the world makes us different or holy.

As I write this, I'm reminded of thousands of Free Methodists from Rwanda, Central Africa. In 1993 long-standing tribal conflict erupted into a campaign of "ethnic cleansing" as the ruling minority Tutsi's sought to wipe out members of the majority Hutu tribe. Two years later tens of thousands of Rwandan Free Methodists had fled to neighboring Zaire and Tanzania. There, as refugees, or "resident aliens," they survived in refugee camps. Despite all their losses—home, possessions, family members—these refugees organized themselves as the People of God. Even in a land where they didn't belong, they remained the church. Ultimately, their identity was not rooted here in this world, but in God.

Dare we ask how much at home *we* are in this world? The question is not so much what we say or claim, but what our lifestyle actually suggests about where we've planted roots—in this world or in God. Consider, if the stock market crashes and our economy lies in ruins, what then? If we're passed over for the promotion, how about that? If our sons and daughters leave town and church to be missionaries halfway around the world? If the government revokes the tax deduction for charitable contributions, what happens to our ministry budgets? If we were actually run from native soil, would we establish the church as one of the first orders of business? Who are our heroes, and our children's—rock musicians and the superstars of professional sports, or Mother Teresa and Billy Graham, and others like them?

Even if we are "aliens" and don't belong in this world, we still spend a good bit of time here. Why do we remain even after God has made us "aliens"? Why doesn't He whisk us to heaven where we belong the moment we believe?

ALIENS ON A MISSION

Our answer is that we are followers of Jesus. Through Him we've been given new birth to an inheritance not of this world (1 Peter 1:3-5). And, God is at work to make us like Jesus as we follow Him. Jesus had a mission and so do we. Peter clarifies our mission as followers of Jesus in a world that is not our home.

As you come to Him, the living Stone—rejected by men but chosen by God and precious to Him—you also, like living stones, are being built into a spiritual house to be a holy priesthood, offering spiritual sacrifices acceptable to God through Jesus Christ (1 Peter 2:4-5).

Peter describes our Christian lives as "coming to Jesus." The present tense suggests that in one sense the whole of life is a coming to, or approaching, Jesus. In our initial commitment to Him as Savior and Lord, we came to Him. But in our everyday lives we come again and again to Him. Certainly the nitty-gritty experiences of life show us our need of Him, and provide us opportunity to come ever closer.

Peter says that "coming to Jesus" makes us like Him. If Jesus is the "living Stone," we become like "living stones." And, if Jesus becomes the "chosen and precious cornerstone" of God's spiritual house, we become the materials God uses in building the house. "You are being built into a spiritual house" (v. 5). A *house* shelters people and becomes a home. A *spiritual house* offers welcome and refuge to people and makes them the family of God.

One facet of our mission, then, is to become a place for people to be family. How desperately our world needs this. Loneliness, brokenness, and isolation often invade modern life. Economic crisis and unemployment routinely force people to live "on the street." Spouse and child abuse leave victims wounded and hurting. Restlessness and dissatisfaction prompt multiple career changes and households move here and there. Family life breaks down with epidemic frequency through divorce or lifestyle choices that drive a wedge between parents and children. These features of modern life hinder many from developing deep and satisfying relationships. All around us are people who need a place, a community, a family where they can be at home. Peter says that as we come to Jesus, God is at work to make us a people who offer the safety and joy of His family to others. Our mission calls for allowing God to form His household among us.

BECOMING FAMILY

If we take this mission seriously, we will develop and experience church as the family of God. Our churches will be home for people whose experiences in the world have left them physically, emotionally, and spiritually homeless. I think at least two agenda items suggest themselves for the church.

■ First, we must make sure that we are in fact family, that our fellowship is fellowship (see chapters 11 and 12 for a full account of what this involves). We must take care that our programs and ministries, and the mood or climate of our people, communicate a welcome. In some cases this may be accomplished simply by directing and shaping what is already happening in the church. Yet, underneath this climate of loving acceptance must be vital spiritual reality. The church needs to recognize this as the true mark of the church and seek the grace to be authentic at this point. A good test is to observe what happens when members fall on hard times. "Family" will be there for its own and will help, even to the point of sacrifice. A second test is to ask whether the church would offer such care to those not yet on the inside.

■ Second, the church as a whole and each of the church's sub-groupings can become intentional about identifying the homeless in the surrounding community.

What are their needs? How can we offer them family? And, then, the church can design whatever ministries are needed. These may be cooperative ventures with other churches or organizations. Perhaps they will even form partnerships with government agencies, locally and nationally. The current approach to social problems almost guarantees that the ranks of the poor among us will increase in the next several decades. The church's mission as "family" couldn't be more relevant.

A FAMILY OF PRIESTS

Changing his imagery, Peter also says we become a "holy priesthood." That is, we are home for a family of priests. As priests we represent God and His concerns to others, helping them make connection with God. When Peter says we "offer spiritual sacrifices acceptable to God through Jesus Christ," he draws a comparison and a contrast with the priesthood of the Old Testament. Like the Old Testament model, we offer sacrifices to God that are pleasing to Him. Unlike the Old Testament model, we do not offer animals or produce, but *people*.

Our mission, therefore, has both an inward and an outward thrust. We are called to nurture a sense of family where God is at home with us and we are at home with Him. This is not an exclusive family, but one of "priests" who embrace the world and help others make living connection with God.

Peter expresses the same twofold mission in other terms, "But you are a chosen people, a royal priesthood, a holy nation, a people belonging to God, that you may declare the praises of Him who called you out of darkness into His wonderful light" (1 Peter 2:9). When we come to Jesus and follow Him, we become God's holy people who belong completely to Him. That's the inward thrust of our mission—to be a holy family. But we are His people not simply for our pleasure, but for His purposes—to make Him and His plan known to others. That's the outward thrust of our mission—to be a holy priesthood.

This vision of our life together as holy people calls us to consider carefully how we relate to one another as fellow believers and to the world around us. Indeed, taking what Peter says seriously challenges us deeply. We are called to be the *family of God,* and that calling must be the starting point for any talk of "family values." Our first sense of belonging, after our relationship with God, should be the belonging we sense with one another as brothers and sisters in Christ.

Consider the clear teachings of Jesus on this matter. When He learned that His mother and brothers had come to talk with Him, probably because people were beginning to wonder about His strange behavior, Jesus asked, "'Who is My mother, and who are My brothers?' Pointing to His disciples, He said, 'Here are My mother and My brothers. For whoever does the will of My Father in heaven is My brother and sister and mother'" (Matthew 12:48-50). Belonging to one another in Him takes priority even over our biological families! In fact, our biological families may become one of the greatest hindrances to our being His followers. Jesus cautioned that, for some, the decision to follow Him may cause conflict, even the breakdown of the family unit:

> Do you think I come to bring peace on earth? No, I tell you, but division. From now on there will be five in one family divided against each other, three against two and two against three. They will be divided, father against son and son against father, mother against daughter and

125

daughter against mother, mother-in-law against daughter-in-law and daughter-in-law against mother-in-law (Luke 12:51-53).

Jesus listed among the rigorous demands of discipleship, "If anyone comes to Me and does not hate his father and mother, his wife and children, his brothers and sisters—yes, even his own life—he cannot be My disciple" (Luke 14:26). Of course, Jesus' point is not that we are actually to hate our loved ones or despise ourselves. Rather, our commitment to follow Him must take priority over every other commitment in this life. Even the most important and sacred of these—to our family— is no exception to this rule.

But what about our responsibility to the family God has given us? Does Jesus call us to ignore them? Aren't His demands dangerous, especially in our Western culture where many families suffer abuse and all kinds of dysfunction? And, doesn't this reading of the cost of discipleship conflict with other clear teachings from the Scriptures? After all, in both Old and New Testaments we are commanded to take special responsibility for our biological families (see Deuteronomy 6:1-9, Ephesians 6:4, as well as other passages).

Several observations have helped me sort out these matters. First, I recall that Jesus took special care of His own mother. From the cross He committed her care to His beloved disciple (see John 19:26-27). Obviously, then, being like Jesus and being the Family of God will not lead us to refuse loving care to our families. Second, in both Testaments, family units were not regarded as separated from, but part of, the larger community of God's people. The commands to nurture family always have full participation in the People of God as its goal. Certainly, the most important responsibility we have to our individual family members is to encourage their entrance into God's family. Jesus does not call for less family, but for more. He would draw us into larger and deeper family connection than would ever be possible on merely human terms. In fact, though following Jesus may lead to the loss of family in some sense, He promised 100 percent more in mothers and fathers and brothers and sisters in this life (see Mark 10:29-30)! Jesus' call does not diminish family life, but expands and enriches it!

Yet, as we've seen, our mission to be family as the people of God challenges us to belong so fully to God that we actually exist not for ourselves, or for our own family, but for God and others. Exclusive relationships with our individual families and friends and the busyness of our lives that requires neglect of family and church both signal unholiness. Instead, we are called to deep involvement in one another's lives, to a kind of sharing and caring, that will have a family feel to it, and to a spirit of oneness that will attract others to God's Family. Our mission requires us to make adjustments so that we are, in fact, the Spiritual Household God wants us to be.

A NEW PEOPLE

Our mission also challenges the place of the family in the culture of the secular world and of the conservative church world. Much of the secular world has minimal requirements for a group to be a family, and then pushes and pressures families to the point of disintegration. In response to this cultural reality, we champion the biblical vision of lifelong heterosexual marriage and responsible parenthood. We insist that the home, as God created it, is basic to human well-being, and deserving of care and protection.

The subculture of some conservative Christians sometimes views the family as the primary goal of Christian life, and makes marriage and parental duty an obligation second only to what we owe God. In response to this cultural view, we should champion the biblical vision of the People of God as the divinely ordained context of a Christ-centered family. While we have special responsibilities toward the families God has entrusted to us, we will fulfill them better when they are cultured in the community of God's people.

In truth, our mission to be a priesthood—to help others make connection with God—depends on our being the church family God calls us to be. When God forms us into this family, we reflect the beauty, order, and love for which broken and hurting people long. If we accept our mission, all sorts of people will be drawn to what they see among us. And what we tell them about God will have convincing power.

Through these three images—*alien, family,* and *priesthood*—Peter shows us that following Jesus draws us together as a new kind of people who live in the world not for ourselves but for God and others. *Internally,* we allow God to make us family; we share together the joys and sorrows of life; we care for one another in times of need; and we become a people among whom the living God beautifully dwells. *Externally,* we are eager to show and tell others what God has done for us. We penetrate the world to find, welcome, and embrace hurting and lost people who need the healing and health that comes only by being at home with God.

I recall again the thousands of Free Methodist refugees driven from their homes in Rwanda to neighboring countries. Many of them lost everything but life itself. Yet, they found one another in their exile and reorganized themselves as the Family of God. In one of their letters to the States, a group of these refugees thanked the American church for their love and prayers during their exile. Then they requested that special offerings be taken to meet several of their most pressing needs. They asked for Bibles, hymnals, chalkboards, and sound systems. That may seem like a strange wish list for people in their situation, but not really. They are God's holy people and they have a mission. Having established their sense of family in the Spirit, they've now turned their attention to the thousands around them who need to know about Jesus. They are exiles, God's spiritual household, and a holy priesthood. Together they demonstrate and declare what God can do for all people.

ABSTAIN FROM EVIL DESIRES

Obviously, a holy people accomplishes their mission from God together. We cannot be the family of God by ourselves and we cannot be a holy priesthood in isolation. But that does not mean we have no individual responsibilities in carrying out the mission. In fact, Peter insists we will never become the people God calls us to be, nor fulfill our mission, without tending to our individual responsibilities. He summarizes them as follows:

> Dear friends, I urge you, as aliens and strangers in the world, to abstain from sinful desires, which war against your soul. Live such good lives among the pagans that, though they accuse you of doing wrong, they may see your good deeds and glorify God on the day He visits us (1 Peter 2:11-12).

129

Peter urges each of us to accept a twofold mandate which speaks to the inner unity (family) and outer thrust (priesthood) of our mission. First, he calls us to "abstain" or stay away from sinful desires. Most modern people do not like negatives or prohibitions. We'd like to find a positive way to say it, or not say it at all, especially when it comes to spiritual matters. But some prohibitions simply must be heard. We tell our children not to touch the burners on the stove. We expect companies to warn us of any dangers associated with the products they make. Peter warns us about sinful desires and tells us to reject them.

We all have desires, longings, and appetites; while most of these are not sinful in themselves, all of them can be perverted and twisted toward sinful ends. I suppose most of us think of sexual desire as the most common example of this. Because God created us as sexual beings, human sexuality is positively right and good! It played an important role in the original creation that God called *very good* (Genesis 1:31). But sexual desire often becomes sinful. Because it is one of God's most wonderful gifts, our enemy, the devil, takes delight when it is misused. The greater the gift and the greater the joy it brings us, the more Satan seeks to pervert it, and us in the process. That's why holiness language in the Bible is often used in relation to sexuality (see 1 Corinthians and 1 Thessalonians). By attacking us at the point of sexual desire, the enemy hopes to rob us of God's good gift and keep us from being the unique people of God.

God intended our sexual drive to draw us to the one person to whom we commit ourselves in marriage. Sexual intercourse should be the expression of love and intimacy between husband and wife. Yet, often, sexual desire becomes selfish and is employed as a tool to coerce others. Through sex people use one another as objects of pleasure. The sinful corruption of sexuality leads to the very opposite of true love.

But there are other desires, natural to us as creatures of God but often perverted by sin. We think of our desires for attention, accomplishment, pleasure, entertainment, security, convenience, comfort, competence, and knowledge. All of these, though quite natural, can become sinful. Peter says that believers should abstain, have nothing to do with sinful desires or longings.

How do we know when a desire should be resisted and rejected because it is sinful? Peter answers that they make war against the soul. He's not talking about "soul" in the sense of a hidden, invisible part of you as a person. In the Bible "soul" refers primarily to the capacity we have for a relationship with God. Here's the principle: anything that draws you away from God, rather than closer to Him, anything that cools your affection for Jesus, that does not help you become more like Him, anything that stands in the way of doing what God wants you to do is to be avoided.

You and I recognize a sinful desire when we see one. Among the most common are a fascination with entertainment promoting sexuality outside God's will, an enticing desire to have more than we do and be discontent with what we have, the drive to excel at the expense of others, the urge to repay evil with evil. In addition to these common sinful desires, each of us can list others that especially threaten to make us less than the holy people of God. And, lest we fear being unaware of threatening sinful desires, the Holy Spirit promises to reveal them to us.

Peter urges us to abstain from all sinful desires. However strong they may be, we can steer clear of them.

Remember, Jesus has redeemed us or set us free from these very desires and the way of life they represent. "You know that it was not with perishable things such as silver or gold that you were redeemed from the empty way of life handed down to you from your forefathers, but with the precious blood of Christ, a lamb without blemish or defect" (1 Peter 1:18-19). Precisely because Jesus has set us free, we can rid ourselves "of all malice and all deceit, hypocrisy, envy, and slander of every kind" (1 Peter 2:1). For "He Himself bore our sins in His body on the tree, so that we might die to sins and live for righteousness; by His wounds you have been healed" (1 Peter 2:24).

People don't slip away from God "by accident." Nor is there any such thing as spiritual kidnapping. Falling away is the result of choices we have made, desires we embraced, that created distance between us and God. Peter *assures* us this need never happen. We *can* abstain. On the basis of Jesus' death and resurrection, the Spirit empowers us to reject *all* sinful desires.

God works directly in our lives supplying the strength we need; He also works indirectly through "the means of grace," wonderful gifts to His Family that nourish us. Through the Scriptures, prayer, sharing with other believers, worship, and serving others, God strengthens us to reject sinful desires and grow in our relationship with Him.

We are either walking away from God or toward God. Peter urges us to move toward God, coming ever closer, to stay away from anything or anyone who hinders us from drawing near. As we draw near we are taking care of our souls, so that *together* with our brothers and sisters in the Lord, God can form us into His Family.

LIVE WELL AMONG THE PAGANS

The second half of Peter's mandate for accomplishing our mission calls us to live "good lives among the pagans." He takes it for granted that we will interact with unbelievers. Holiness has often been misunderstood as a call to have no contact with unbelieving people, especially if they live in blatant immorality. Indeed, some branches of the Christian church have made a specialty of disassociating from the unsavory elements of society. But clearly that's not the way of Jesus. Ironically, disassociation in the name of holiness may actually be a sign of unholiness! Any brand of "holy living" that keeps us from interaction with those who most need God's love is foreign to the way of Jesus.

To be sure, the Bible calls God's people to be different from unbelievers, but we are to be different in the way Jesus was, because *He* is the basic model of holiness. While Jesus established close friendship ties and deep fellowship only with His disciples and His family, He was constantly among people of all types. He got close enough to know their names and histories, close enough so that they could know Him and want to come even closer!

Our mission as holy people requires us to follow our Lord, Peter insists. We must interact with unbelievers enough for them to see who we are, what kind of stuff we're made of, how we react to people and circumstances. Especially when we're under fire, experiencing adversity, mistreated by others, falsely accused, we must be close enough so they will see our responses. And when they do, Peter says, many will be attracted. They will wonder about Jesus and be drawn to the God who makes us Family and employs us as priests in the world. On the final day, many of them will join us in praising God.

THE STRATEGIC CHURCH

To be like Jesus and to live a holy life requires us to interact with unbelievers so they can see Jesus in us. While that's a challenge each of us must meet individually, part of the church's mission must be to encourage us to meet the challenge. Our leaders need to model interaction with unbelievers. Their example not only shows us how to do it, but sends a powerful message to the Body that this is what its members do.

Having created a climate where such interaction becomes the norm, the church can give members "permission" or encouragement to develop their gifts and abilities in order to make an impact on their world. We must help one another understand that God calls people to be "priestly" librarians, custodians, homemakers, accountants, physicians, nurses, attorneys, teachers, or construction workers. In every field of endeavor, unbelievers need the ministry of the priestly people of God.

The church needs to have the mind-set of a missionary task force. Within the family fellowship, members are formed, trained, equipped, confirmed, commissioned, and deployed as missionaries during the week. Church will become not so much a place to which we come but a place from which we go to do our mission as the holy people of God. The church should consider changing its vocabulary, modifying its schedules, and altering its programs to become truly "mission-al."

What a priestly mission! God calls us individually and collectively to penetrate the world as members of His Family in such a way that many will take note, see in us something real and authentic, and turn toward

God. This mission does not aim to restructure society, resolve great social and moral plagues, or reform human government. Yet, in spiritually subversive ways, as we pursue our mission, God will bring transformation in all of these areas. As we model Jesus' way of life, we will be offering a radical alternative to the world's ways on which current social, political, and cultural reality rests. When God's people accomplish their mission, transformation occurs, not only within individuals but also within society.

Notice that both halves of the mandate must be observed in order to accept our mission. Caring for our personal relationship with God, abstaining from all that hinders us and drawing ever closer to God, is essential if we are to live the "good lives" that will impact the unbelieving world. And, obviously, we must be close enough to unbelieving people so that this impact can indeed occur! Being God's holy people calls for a balance between internal care for our souls and external interaction with unbelievers.

Maintaining that balance is a challenge. In most churches people tend to rally around one half of the mandate as if it were either/or. Either we focus on things we do at church or we meet people's needs in the community. Either we're content to be in the sanctuary or we work in the soup kitchen. Either we cultivate our walk with the Lord or we let our lights shine in the marketplace.

However, when it becomes either/or, we're just a step away from neither/nor. When it's neither/nor, the church will be neither the Family nor the Priesthood He desires. Let's not forget that we're seeking to be like Jesus. He was one with His Father-God, yet constantly interacting with people, drawing them to a new life.

MISSION IMPOSSIBLE

In the TV program the tape recorded message outlining the mission always concluded with a summary that began, "Your mission, should you decide to accept it, is ... ." In one sense, there *was* a choice, and yet, we all knew there was no *real* choice, not if the Director was telling the truth and if Jim and his cohorts were the sort of people we believed them to be. There was no question that they would accept the mission and accomplish it. The only question was about the creative strategies these agents would employ to accomplish their mission. That's what made each episode so exciting.

It's the same for us as the holy people of God. Our Director tells us the truth as He calls us to accept a mission of life and death and eternal consequence. We *do* have a choice. Yet, if we are the people God calls us to be, the people we claim to be, there is no *real* choice. Nor is there any question about the ultimate outcome of the mission. Accomplishment is certain.

But isn't this mission truly impossible, especially for the likes of us, and especially for the church as we know it? Can we really expect to become a Family of brothers and sisters in Christ whose belonging to each other takes priority over every other sort of human belonging? Can we truly envision being such a Family, not waiting for others to come to us but moving out in mission with eagerness to serve people everywhere with priestly devotion?

The mission God calls us to accept as His holy people does not depend on *our* ingenuity and creativity. We're called to follow Jesus. When He began His mission, He cited the words of Isaiah, "The Spirit of the Lord is on Me because He has anointed Me ..." (Luke 4:18). It was in the power of the Spirit of God that the Son of God accomplished His mission. Similarly, when Jesus conferred the mission upon His followers, He promised them that the Spirit would come upon them and empower them to accomplish their mission.

The book of Acts begins to tell the story. When the Spirit came upon the followers of Jesus on the day of Pentecost, they proclaimed the mighty deeds of God (Acts 2:1-13). By the Spirit's gift their proclamation drew people from all over the world. Before the day was over, those very people had become a new kind of Family, and their close, caring fellowship attracted new folk on a daily basis and made them at home with God (Acts 2, 3, 4). We also read about the awesome work of the Spirit in their family fellowship that caused them to reach out to others with power, to meet every sort of human need, and to see others join the family.

This was a fellowship that embraced people of all ethnic and cultural backgrounds and that offered daring forgiveness and acceptance even to Saul of Tarsus, a former enemy who was now a brother (Acts 9:10-19, 26-30; Galatians 1:18-24). Although not perfect, the early church became a family, the likes of which the world had never seen—a family of strangers and aliens, seeking the welfare of all people with priestly devotion.

Our mission is not impossible because we have access to the same Spirit of God. His power makes Jesus' mandate not a mission impossible, but a mission to be accomplished. Let the church wait and pray and seek the fullness of God's Spirit, and let the world beware!

CHAPTER TEN

Facing the Reality of Suffering

don't know about you, but I hate "fine print"! More often than I care to admit, I've signed up for some great deal only to learn that things were not what they seemed. Of course, the fine print at the bottom, which even eagles couldn't see without corrective lenses, told the whole story. Perhaps you've had experiences like the following.

■ While leafing through the newspaper, an ad catches your eye. It announces super-saver fares for flights from coast to coast, a promotional campaign for a new airline company. Unbelievably, $39.00 each way from New York to Los Angeles. But then, you notice an asterisk. Below you find the matching asterisk and with a squint you read, "The following restrictions apply: four-year advance purchase; must travel on a Monday between 3:10 and 3:15 a.m., on odd months of a leap year; subject to availability; prices may change without notice."

■ At Christmastime your child's dream gift comes in a package with the small warning, "Some Assembly Required." Experience tells you only engineers need bother. In truth, the box contains just a collection of spare parts from the factory floor, which also explains why the price was such a steal!

■ Once I saw an announcement in the paper about a new way to buy used cars. By phone! I had to read it twice to make sure I hadn't misunderstood—I was just a phone call away from a new set of wheels. Then, at the bottom, in fine print I read, "When you call please ask for our sales representative, Mr. Hurt." Something inside me whispered, "The name is prophetic—get involved with him and it will hurt!" I hate fine print!

When we sign on to follow Jesus we don't need to worry about hidden messages. Everything is out in the open, written in large print. According to the New Testament, following Jesus will lead to controversy, conflict, and suffering. On one occasion, a teacher of Moses' law eagerly offered to join Jesus' disciples. But Jesus responded, "Foxes have holes and birds of the air have nests, but the Son of Man has no place to lay His head" (Matthew 8:20). In other words, "Join me and it could cost you everything. Still interested?"

Toward the end of His ministry, Jesus' call to discipleship actually became a call to join Him on the way of suffering. Jesus began to explain to His disciples that He must go to Jerusalem and suffer many things. When Peter protested the very idea of a suffering Messiah, Jesus rebuked him as being in league with Satan, and issued an invitation to suffer with Him by taking up the cross and following (see Matthew 16:21-28).

Jesus wasn't joking. Within weeks of Pentecost, when the early church was established, Peter and John were arrested for disturbing the peace. God had used them to heal a disabled man at the Temple gate. The miracle nearly led to a riot, and Peter and John were fingered as the culprits. Because it was late in the day, they had to spend the night in jail. That would have been suffering enough, but the next day the authorities summoned them to explain their seditious behavior. The same people had examined Jesus, and you know where that led! The authorities bullied them, threatening dire consequences if they ever again taught or spoke in the name of Jesus (see Acts 3:1-4:22). Unjust arrest, a stay in the local dungeon, an appearance before the supreme court that had just murdered the Son of God, and an order to cease and desist or else—sounds like a recipe for "suffering stew."

But that suffering was mild compared to what lay ahead for the early Christians. Stephen had been chosen to manage the food pantry in Jerusalem, but the Holy Spirit had other ideas. His practical ministries were complemented by a strong preaching witness for Jesus, so strong that his opponents in the city flew into a rage and murdered him by stoning. Stephen's murder then ignited a citywide campaign to drive all followers of Jesus out of town, if not out of this world (see Acts 6:8-7:60).

Sometimes we think of such opposition and violence against Christians as unusual. In truth, however, it was more the rule than the exception. Acts' story of the early church paints a picture filled with pain and suffering for the followers of Jesus. Besides Stephen's martyrdom, James, the brother of John, suffered execution by Herod (Acts 12:1-2).

PAUL AND PETER

One of the great ironies of the early church's suffering may be seen in the life of Paul. He began his religious career as a duly appointed persecutor of believers, at one time cursing and threatening followers of Jesus as naturally as he breathed (see Acts 9:1). But once Paul met Jesus and began to follow Him, the Lord showed him "how much he must suffer for My name" (Acts 9:16). Paul describes his ministry in brutal language.

> We are hard pressed on every side, but not crushed; perplexed, but not in despair; persecuted, but not abandoned; struck down, but not destroyed. We always carry around in our body the death of Jesus ... For we who are alive are always being given over to death for Jesus' sake (2 Corinthians 4:8-11).

When other so-called apostles listed their accomplishments, highlighting the miraculous, Paul stressed how his ministry had been punctuated with pain.

> Five times I received from the Jews the forty lashes minus one. Three times I was beaten with rods, once I was stoned, three times I was shipwrecked, I spent a night and a day in the open sea, I have been constantly on the move. I have been in danger from rivers ... bandits ... my own countrymen ... Gentiles ... in the city ... in the country ... at sea, and in danger from false brothers. I have labored and toiled and have often gone without sleep; I have known hunger and thirst and have often gone without food; I have been cold and naked ... (2 Corinthians 11:24-27).

Paul knew that following Jesus would lead to experiencing what Jesus did. By the end of his life he had come to a firm conclusion on suffering and the Christian way. "In fact, everyone who wants to live a godly life in Christ Jesus will be persecuted" (2 Timothy 3:12). As we shall see, Paul's experience and conclusion are more the rule than the exception for all followers of Jesus.

First, however, a clarification. Followers of Jesus,

like all people, often suffer simply because they are human and live in a world where bad things happen. I recall a seven-month period in the life of our church when two families suffered the loss of newborns. Strangely, both children had somehow contracted the same rare bacterial infection. The parents' suffering was intense. Almost daily such stories assault our sense of justice and burden our hearts. All people share this common experience of uninvited and unmerited suffering.

In addition to these common human experiences of pain, there is a form of suffering for followers of Jesus, simply because they follow Him. Peter says, "Do not be surprised at the painful trial you are suffering, as though something strange were happening to you" (1 Peter 4:12). We might paraphrase this, "Remember, when Jesus called us to follow, there was no fine print. This is just what we expected!" The early church viewed suffering for the sake of Jesus as a powerful confirmation that their faith was genuine (compare 1 Thessalonians 1:9 with 1 Peter 1:6-7). At the end of his letter Peter wrote, "Your brothers throughout the world are undergoing the same kind of sufferings" (1 Peter 5:9).

What kind of suffering did Peter have in mind? There was the suffering of slaves whose masters had no regard for God. These violent men enjoyed treating their slaves cruelly, especially those who confessed faith in Christ. There were women among Peter's first readers who suffered as well. They came to faith but their husbands didn't. In the first century world, a religiously divided home often became a battlefield, leaving the woman wounded or worse. These wives could be thrown out and lose home, children, and all means of support. If they took their faith less seriously, conditions would improve immediately (see 1 Peter 2:18-25 and 3:1-6).

HOLINESS MEANS SUFFERING

At the beginning of his letter, Peter describes his Christian readers with holiness language, telling them they are "God's elect, strangers in the world ... through *the sanctifying work of the Spirit*" (1 Peter 1:1-2, emphasis added). To "sanctify" means "to make, or set apart as, holy." The sanctifying work of the Spirit makes people holy.

Early in his letter Peter urged, "As obedient children, do not conform to the evil desires you had when you lived in ignorance. But just as He who called you is holy, so be holy in all you do; for it is written, 'Be holy, because I am holy'" (1 Peter 1:14-16). In the life of all true followers of Jesus, God's Spirit is at work to make them like God. Since that is true, they should embrace what God is doing and refuse to return to their former, ungodly patterns of life. Being holy means being different. Just as God is not like other gods or powers, so His people are not to be like other people.

And what happens to people who are different? Your ten-year-old comes home from school complaining about his clothes. When he left to catch the bus in the morning, he couldn't have cared less what he was wearing. But now he cares. His clothing is not like what the other kids are wearing, and they made fun of him and made him feel lousy.

Watch carefully what happens the next time you're in a crowded room and someone wheels in a severely handicapped person. Immediately the atmosphere changes. No one looks directly at the disabled person, though everyone steals side glances when it seems safe to do so. If people were laughing, they suddenly become serious. If people were talking, they may lose their train of thought. Perhaps a child innocently blurts out,

"Daddy, what's wrong with *her?*" Of course, most of us would never dream of hurting the disabled person. Yet, almost always, the person in the wheelchair observes these reactions and finds them painful. Because she is different, she suffers.

My wife grew up in southeastern Ohio near a thriving Amish community. Hers was the only "English" (non-Amish) family in their little village. Through the years she became friends with many of her Amish neighbors. Sadly, however, these cordial relations could not be taken for granted. Several years ago, an Amish buggy was run off the road by a car, and a little girl lost her life in the accident. Unfortunately, such accidents occur too often, despite the frequent yellow caution signs with the buggy on them. In the weeks that followed this incident, the investigation uncovered the shocking truth that it wasn't accidental. The young people in the car, bored on a Friday night, decided to find some Amish to harass.

That's the way it is with followers of Jesus. There is no fine print! Since they are holy, which means different from others, and since the world around them *is* hostile to people who are different, they *will* suffer. Let's consider three reasons why they will suffer.

FOLLOWERS OF JESUS BELONG ONLY TO GOD

You've heard the expression, "Be your own person." Being your *own* person may qualify as a cardinal rule for those who want "to have it all together"! But it's a rule regularly broken by the followers of Jesus. They prefer, "Be *God's* person."

By rights all persons belong to God who created them and therefore has exclusive ownership rights over them. Yet, in their natural state most people have no clue as to whose they are. And they also have no clue that what they imagine as freedom—trying to be their own person—actually qualifies as a form of slavery. But it's a fact! Consider how the Apostle Paul describes our natural life,

> You were dead in your transgressions and sins, in which you used to live when you followed the ways of this world and of the ruler of the kingdom of the air, the spirit who is now at work in those who are disobedient. All of us also lived among them at one time, gratifying the cravings of our sinful nature and following its desires and thoughts (Ephesians 2:1-3).

Created to be God's, we somehow became slaves, captives to an alien spirit and destructive ways of life. Even our most emphatic declarations of independence and energetic attempts at self-liberation only drive us further from true freedom.

What we cannot do for ourselves, however, God has already done for us through Jesus. As Peter says, "You were redeemed from the empty way of life handed down to you from your forefathers ... with the precious blood of Christ" (1 Peter 1:18-19). God rescued us from a life of trying to do our own thing, live as we desire, and serve as CEO of our lives. We need rescuing from that kind of life because, in the long run, it leads to what we really *don't* want—emptiness, brokenness, hopelessness, and death.

Jesus died and rose from the dead to free us from a life that leads nowhere. It was as though we'd been held captive by terrorists; just as a SWAT team decisively outmaneuvers and overpowers the terrorists, so He has set us free. Free not to be our own persons, but God's. Free to be as He created us to be—in a loving relationship with the only One who makes us truly alive.

It always disrupts "the system" and its keepers—whether at work or among your peers—when you, as a follower of Jesus, are not afraid to break ranks, when you do not slavishly conform to every expectation. More than disrupt, it makes people mad. Your nonconformity will lead them to pressure you. "Perhaps you can be persuaded," they think. But followers of Jesus do not buckle under persuasive pressures. No one owns them but God.

FOLLOWERS OF JESUS LET GOD DIRECT THEIR LIVES

Those who don't own you don't tell you what to do. Nor do you look to them as models and examples for everyday life. Instead, you look to and learn from God, as Jesus reveals Him. Let's consider how following God's direction will likely lead to suffering.

■ Good exposes evil. Because we have been rescued from dead-end living, we have no obligation to walk on dead-end paths. So, Peter urges, don't allow your lives to be controlled by sinful human desires (see 1 Peter 1:14; 2:11). We are free to say "No" to whatever is not good. Likewise, we are free to say "Yes" to the good.

How angry people become when they learn that their way of life is not good. It's not that you make it a point to tell them, but that you live in a way which shows them. Jesus explained why people in His day rejected Him as the light of the world—He said they loved darkness because their deeds were evil (John 3:19). When Jesus came near they were exposed. Sometimes exposure leads people to embrace the light, but they may also try to snuff out the light! As we are like Jesus they may do the same to us!

■ Joyful suffering may increase hostility. When

people experience hardship and suffering, they often complain and grumble, and poison the atmosphere. But even in adversity, followers of Jesus are free to say "No" to the expectations of others and "Yes" to God's direction in their lives. Peter makes a special point of this. Even though believers suffer simply because they are different, rather than complain, they rejoice.

> In this [new birth to a living hope] you greatly rejoice, though now for a little while you may have had to suffer grief in all kinds of trials (1 Peter 1:6).

> But rejoice that you participate in the sufferings of Christ, so that you may be overjoyed when His glory is revealed (1 Peter 4:13).

> However, if you suffer as a Christian, do not be ashamed, but praise God that you bear that name (1 Peter 4:16).

Followers of Jesus have a deep conviction that they and their circumstances are headed to an encounter with ultimate good. Because they are *God's* people and God is ultimately good, when it's all said and done God will win big time. Those who follow Jesus already know the final outcome, and it makes them smile or laugh, even through tears.

When others observe that sort of joy, they will do one of two things. Either they will want the same joy for themselves, or they will try to slap that smile off your face. Either they will follow Jesus, or they will want to make His followers sorry!

■ Following Jesus' example in suffering may lead to still more suffering. Even in painful times of suffering, followers of Jesus are free to break with ordinary human patterns of response and embrace the cross as God's power to transform them through love. As a result they can treat others with the same love and grace God has shown them, responding to aggressors in the way Jesus responded to His. Peter encouraged his readers who were household slaves to follow Jesus' example when their masters mistreated them.

> To this you were called, because Christ suffered for you, leaving you an example, that you should follow in His steps. "He committed no sin, and no deceit was found in His mouth." When they hurled their insults at Him, He did not retaliate; when He suffered, He made no threats. Instead, He entrusted Himself to Him who judges justly (1 Peter 2:21-23).

To be sure, this is hard counsel; indeed, impossible without God's help. But God offers us all the help we need through Jesus' death and resurrection and the Holy Spirit's empowering. Perhaps we're tempted to think that if we respond to suffering the way Jesus did, things will improve. However, that does not always happen. Yet, no matter the response, followers of Jesus let God alone direct their lives. That's holiness, and that's why they suffer.

FOLLOWERS OF JESUS LIVE WITH ETERNAL PERSPECTIVE

Peter tells his readers that their lives are part of an eternal plan. God loves us and has taken action for us through Jesus to give us a new life, not just for here and now, but forever. Consider the sweeping scope of God's plan in sending Jesus and calling us to follow Him:

> He was chosen before the creation of the world, but was revealed in these last times for your sake.

Through Him you believe in God, who raised Him from the dead and glorified Him, and so your faith and hope are in God (1 Peter 1:20-21).

And the God of all grace, who called you to His eternal glory in Christ, after you have suffered a little while, will Himself restore you and make you strong, firm, and steadfast. To Him be the power forever and ever. Amen (1 Peter 5:10-11).

In His great mercy He has given us new birth into a living hope through the resurrection of Jesus Christ from the dead, and into an inheritance that can never perish, spoil or fade—kept in heaven for you, who through faith are shielded by God's power until the coming of the salvation that is ready to be revealed in the last time (1 Peter 1:3-5).

To follow Jesus in this *entirely new kind of life* is to live "out of the future" and with an eternal perspective. This perspective has been revealed in Jesus, whom we follow. We know He lived for God His Father, suffered and died, was raised, and entered into glory. And, along the way, God accomplished His plan. As it was with Jesus, so it will be with us! He suffered, so we're not surprised to meet with suffering. He triumphed and overcame, so we do not lose hope even in the worst of times. We know that we also will triumph and overcome. And, as we do, we know God will be working His plan through us.

Living with eternal perspective means that followers of Jesus will not be driven by the "projected results" or the "likely outcomes" of their circumstances. When someone says, "If you don't go along with the crowd but insist on marching to a different drummer, then you won't be popular, you won't get ahead, the people who count won't be impressed, you won't make as much money, you'll not have the reputation you might have otherwise, you'll be a nobody, you might make people mad, you might end up dead," followers of Jesus think, "Well, yes, what's your point?"

They think this way because of their eternal perspective. They do not live for here and now, and they do not play for worldly crowds and achievements. They live for eternity and direct their experiences toward the revealed plan of God.

Because of their eternal perspective, followers of Jesus regularly submit to the "Ten Thousand Year Test." Here's how it works. In evaluating the concerns, causes, and circumstances of life, they ask, "Will this matter ten thousand years from now?" If so, they pay close attention, adjust, and even suffer. If not, it's probably a trivial pursuit.

Eternal perspective leads them to care supremely about the things Jesus cared about. They are headed for a day of final glory when Jesus returns. They know that everything in this world not submitted to the Creator God will pass away, and everyone who does not know God's love and rescue in Jesus will meet with ultimate disaster. So, they live to share the praises of God who called them from darkness to light. They live so that others can see Jesus in them.

HOLINESS AND SUFFERING TODAY

When I first met Terry, he worked for a local power plant. One of his duties called for the routine inspection of pressure gauges located around the plant. As long as things ran smoothly these inspections were routine and, well, boring. But if a problem arose, his hourly inspections would prevent disaster.

Terry's co-workers had no use for Christianity, or any faith at all. They branded Terry a pious fool and took every opportunity to make his work-life miserable. One evening they began to ridicule him, lured him into a shoving match, and delayed the next round of pressure gauge inspections. Wouldn't you know it, that evening a rare problem arose. Had Terry been delayed a minute longer his suffering (along with everyone else's for miles around) would have ended in a huge explosion. Instead, Terry "saved the day." But the close call was noted by his supervisors. And guess whose work record now carries a blemish for on-the-job negligence? First, he suffered the ridicule and abuse of his fellow workers. Then *he*, the true victim, is blamed for nearly blowing the place up! If Terry would just "go along to get along" the suffering would end. But Terry remains a follower of Jesus.

All around the world today, more sinister forms of suffering assault committed followers of Jesus. Several letters have come to me in recent weeks highlighting blatant persecution of believers in many nations of the world. One letter reports:

> Seventeen Christians die each hour somewhere in the world for their faith. Christian children are being sold into slavery and some Christians have been crucified on crosses because they have named Christ as their Lord. Other documented examples of suffering and persecution include: vandalism to churches and homes; beatings; threats and intimidation through mail, phone calls, messengers; severe discrimination against wives of targeted men; deportation; confiscation of

Bibles and Christian literature; loss of jobs; disappearances; mysterious loss of life; government spies infiltrating church groups; and denied access to water.[1] Nina Shea, director of the Puebla Program on Religious Freedom, says, "We are not talking about mere discrimination, but real persecution—torture, enslavement, rape, imprisonment, forcible separation of children from parents."[2]

As I write these words the persecuted church in other parts of the world has come into the world's spotlight. Many denominations and parachurch organizations have joined together in a campaign to "shatter the silence" concerning the sufferings of persecuted Christians around the world. Politicians are expressing concern and determination that something be done. Indeed, we should use every opportunity and means available to relieve the sufferings of our persecuted brothers and sisters around the world.

At the risk of misunderstanding, however, I think there is something strange in our proper outrage over the suffering church. What is strange is our shock, as though we were surprised to hear that Christians are suffering for their faith, as though we assumed that the world has moved beyond such hostility to the gospel, or that suffering for one's faith is an extraordinary experience. Yet, historically, suffering has been common for the faithful people of God. Furthermore, our relative lack of suffering in following Jesus may well be a minority experience, when we consider the whole body of Christ throughout the world. Perhaps our more "comfortable" brand of Christian life in the West represents the exception to the rule.

This possibility prompts me to consider some hard questions. Why don't we suffer more than we do? Is it simply because our environment is relatively open and friendly toward faith? If that is the answer, then why have we not made a deeper impact upon our culture for the kingdom? Or, does our relative comfort in following Jesus suggest we have become too accommodating toward our environment? Does our limited suffering signal a lack of holiness?

Since our culture allows us freedom from suffering, compared to others around the world, why don't we see more fruit? Why doesn't the supposed openness toward spiritual things lead the church to an expanding influence for Christ in our society, and to redemptive impact on its ills? Or, are we not a challenge to the status quo, at least not enough to make anyone really mad?

Hard questions, aren't they? They have sent me back to the Scriptures for a refresher course on what it means to follow Jesus. Even a quick review reminds me that following *Him* makes us different; in a world that rejects Jesus, *that* will lead to situations of conflict and suffering. The Scriptures convince me that our comfortable patterns of Christian living and, even more, our surprise at the suffering of others, uncovers a need for God's holy work among us. These hard questions also drive me to prayer—to seek the God whose presence makes us holy, and who will distinguish us clearly from the social, political, moral, and spiritual chaos around us. I have to believe that when God does this work among us, suffering will have a larger place in our lives.

Yet, I am greatly encouraged! I'm convinced that the young people among us are showing us the way. In our own youth ministries, high school students are finding the Lord and determining to live for Him, no matter what. That means they care about their families and friends who do not know Jesus and they witness to them.

That also means they make the adjustments necessary so that following Jesus will be number one in their lives. In some cases, students have given up promising sports involvement in their school so they will be free to make an eternal difference. Such choices often lead their family and friends to accuse them of being fanatics. In some cases friendships are strained or lost. When young people make such choices and bear the bitter consequences gladly, something or Someone remarkable is at work. I believe they offer us a model of radical faith in Jesus.

A couple of years ago several young people decided to follow Jesus through the witness of friends in our youth group. These new Christians came from families that held nominal association with mainline denominations. But when their sons and daughters started eating, sleeping, walking, and talking "Jesus," they became very interested in religion. More specifically, they were concerned about saving their kids from "going off the deep end." As a result, these parents pressured their kids to renounce the faith, or at least to be "more reasonable." They forbade them to go to our church, threatened to kick them out of the house, and bad-mouthed the church as "a sect that was breaking up our family." Both the young converts and the church God used to disciple them *suffered*. Following Jesus seriously led them to a confrontation with real hostility and threat in their daily lives.

I'm encouraged to think of our young people showing us the way. To be sure, many of them are immature and in need of ongoing nurture and guidance. Yet, their devotion to Jesus, and their zeal to be all He wants, no matter the consequence, beckons us all to follow Jesus seriously enough to suffer.

I'm convinced this represents the wave of the future—more, not less suffering. Not because of an end-time drama about to begin, where the Antichrist appears to rid the world of all Christians. Rather, the radical commitment of these young people, making them a challenge to the status quo and leading them to suffering, is the call to holiness or Christlikeness God issues to the church. If we are to have a future, I believe it must rise out of such commitment. It's the only future God offers us.

NO FINE PRINT

Following Jesus as the holy people of God will mean conflict and suffering. Since that is so, why do we want to follow Him? Don't we have enough heartache and suffering as it is, simply because we are human? Why add to it? Three simple answers.

First, it is *Jesus* who calls us. *Jesus!* God's Son loves us enough to die for us. He's the One with infinite wisdom, with deep awareness of who we are and what we're all about. If *He* says, "Come along. It'll be hard, but worth it," we know it must be good.

Second, following Jesus places us in the sweep of an eternal story—from before time to beyond time. We are called to something Big where everything is at stake for us and for others. Walking with Jesus expresses an eternal plan to make God's presence and kingship real for all people and places.

Third, following Jesus assures our participation in His final victory. Even if faithfulness here and now leads to loss, we can't possibly lose. Ten thousand years from now the glory of His victory will make it hard to remember the difficulties of our following.

That leads us to ask how we can follow Jesus in such radical ways. We know ourselves too well. Especially in the West, our love of comfort and ease, and our skills in acquiring them, make it hard for us even to imagine a life flowing out of such radical commitment, not to mention actually living that way. Again, three simple answers.

First, Jesus died and rose again to free us from all that would hinder our following Him faithfully and radically. His dying on the cross liberates us from all sin, including the love of comfort and ease. His resurrection guarantees power to do whatever God asks us to do.

Second, Jesus sends the Holy Spirit to put into effect all He promises us. The Spirit powerfully works to make us aware of our needs, to help us reject our sin, and to seek God for help. Then He empowers us to follow Jesus, no matter what.

Third, Jesus calls us to walk not only with Him but with one another. The community of God's people that we become when we follow Jesus provides a rich and necessary resource for living the holy life. As we will see in our final chapters, God's people are God's gift to us. The community of God's people helps us learn what it means to be holy, affirms us as we receive the empowerment of the Spirit, holds us accountable for how we live, and supports us when we encounter difficulty and suffering. Remember, there's no "fine print"!

CHAPTER ELEVEN

Thriving in Community

I remember the first time each of our three little girls walked. What a thrill for them and for us—partytime for the whole family!

But it didn't just happen. None of our girls, nor any other child, for that matter, simply walks "out of the blue." There were milestones in their physical development that had to be passed. They had to develop to a particular point. Yet, even with the physical requirements met, learning to walk wasn't mastered entirely on their own. We didn't send them to lectures on the dynamics of pedestrian mobility. Nor did they watch a video; and, since they couldn't read, the latest how-to book was no help.

Our girls learned to walk in *community*. These little people saw family members on foot and it made them curious. They observed that walking is faster than crawling and that walking people are up higher and can see and reach more. Soon they decided to give it a try!

Family members encourage their little ones to walk. "Come on, stand up, let go, that's right. Now, take a step. Good!" And when the first faltering steps lead to a tumble, the family is there to pick them up, brush them off, apply Band-Aids, and cheer them when they try again.

Finally, with just a few steps mastered, families make a feature-length film and call grandma and grandpa to share the joy. Yes, children learn to walk within a community of walkers. Without that community, learning would be so much more difficult.

As you may know, the Bible uses "walking" as a figure of speech for living as God's people. Here are some examples:

> And now, O Israel, what does the Lord your God ask of you but to fear the Lord your God, to walk in all His ways ... (Deuteronomy 10:12).

> The Lord will establish you as His holy people, as He promised you on oath, if you keep the commands of the Lord your God and walk in His ways (Deuteronomy 28:9).

> Teach me Your way, O Lord, and I will walk in Your truth (Psalms 86:11).

> Blessed are they whose ways are blameless, who walk according to the law of the Lord (Psalms 119:1).

> This is what the Lord says: "Stand at the crossroads and look; ask for the ancient paths, ask where the good way is, and walk in it" (Jeremiah 6:16).

> When Jesus spoke again to the people, He said, "I am the light of the world. Whoever follows Me will never walk in darkness, but will have the light of life" (John 8:12).

> We were therefore buried with Him through baptism into death in order that, just as Christ was

raised from the dead through the glory of the Father, we too may live a new life [literally, walk in newness of life] (Romans 6:4).

We live [walk] by faith, not by sight (2 Corinthians 5:7).

So I say, live [walk] by the Spirit, and you will not gratify the desires of the sinful nature (Galatians 5:16).

For we are God's workmanship, created in Christ Jesus to do good works, which God prepared in advance for us to do [literally, "that we should walk in" the good works] (Ephesians 2:10).

As a prisoner for the Lord, then, I urge you to live a life [walk] worthy of the calling you have received (Ephesians 4:1).

So I tell you this, and insist on it in the Lord, that you must no longer live [walk] as the Gentiles do, in the futility of their thinking (Ephesians 4:17).

Live a life of [walk in] love, just as Christ loved us ... (Ephesians 5:2).

For you were once darkness, but now you are light in the Lord. Live [walk] as children of light (Ephesians 5:8).

And we pray this in order that you may live a life worthy [walk] of the Lord and may please Him in every way (Colossians 1:10).

But if we walk in the light, as He is in the light, we have fellowship with one another (1 John 1:7).

The Bible writers describe our relationship with God as an ongoing journey, a dynamic comradeship. And when we walk with God we are holy, that is, different from those who don't walk with Him.

Have you ever watched a small child walk and thought, "He walks just like his dad"? This happens quite naturally, whether or not the child intends it. But it can also happen deliberately. I remember the day when our two-year-old began to walk with a limp. So far as we knew she had nothing wrong and so we asked her what was the matter. She said, "Nuthin!" and kept on limping for another week until we finally called the doctor. Fortunately, however, we figured out what was going on before the appointment. Her klutzy father had sprained his ankle the week before. Nothing was wrong; she was just "walking like daddy." Similarly, both naturally and intentionally, followers of Jesus should be learning to walk as Jesus walked.

HOW DO WE LEARN TO WALK?

Little children must find their first steps scary. Likewise, walking like Jesus sounds difficult, even intimidating. We've seen that followers of Jesus trust God no matter what, especially when tough times come. They recognize the things that would ruin their relationship with God and reject them. Similarly, they understand what will enhance their relationship with God. Jesus' followers hang tough and bear up under pressure. Though they suffer insults from others, they love even their enemies and find ways to show them God's goodness.

How do they learn such things? Just as we cannot expect infants to walk, talk, and relate to others on their own, so we cannot reasonably expect people to follow Jesus fully on their own. If they are going to live a holy life, they will need support, encouragement, and help from others. Everyone needs community.

The early Christians would never have questioned their need for community. It was a foregone conclusion that all people would be taught and powerfully shaped by the group to which they belonged. And, in turn, individuals would help shape the others who belonged to their group. In fact, belonging to others was the foundation for personal identity and life.

How strange this sounds to modern ears! Some modern folks insist that the individual, rather than any group, stands at the center of the universe. "Please, I'll do it myself," my children sometimes say to us, and to others whose help they *truly* need.

In contrast, the Bible assumes that we live in *community* and that the *community* plays a critical role in who we are and how we live, for good or ill. Perhaps you've noticed that most of the commands and instructions God gives us in the Bible are in the plural. God addresses us as His people first and only secondarily as individuals. That's not just because the Bible was written to groups; we often speak to groups and make special application to *individual* lives. We do this because our culture prizes individualism and we want to make sure each one understands and applies the truth.

The biblical writers didn't go out of their way to make specific applications to individuals, as we do. That was not because individuals weren't important to them, but because individuals were not all important. The community or the church is the primary target of the Bible's truth, and the writers assumed that they were communicating with all members of the group.

Even more important, the community was and still should be the target of the truth, because the truth comes home to *individuals* most powerfully when heard, received, and lived within the *community*. According to God's Word, we need each other to help us walk, talk, think, act, and react as the holy people of God. On our own we are like children who assume they can do everything by themselves. Of course, it just doesn't work that way.

A couple years ago I joined several others in the great outdoors in hopes of securing pheasant and quail for the dinner table. Beautiful weather and a modest number of birds made for an exciting morning. Then came the accident that still replays in my mind in slow motion. I sighted the game, took aim, squeezed the trigger, and the next thing I knew something was very wrong. When the gun fired I blinked my left eye. A split second later everything—in all directions, both near and far—was a blur. I blinked again, rubbed the eye to remove what I supposed was the irritant, but the blur remained. My right eye saw perfectly, but my left eye was as good as blind!

I reported the accident to my friends and continued to walk through the field a quarter mile to where our cars were parked. The farther we walked the greater my concern, until I reached near panic.

The week before a friend had told me about an injury which I supposed was similar to mine. A small splinter of metal had lodged in his eye. At first he thought he could "blink through" the injury, but he ended up in the hospital having the eye irrigated, which proved very painful!

Now I too anticipated spending the rest of that Saturday in the emergency room. I thought, "Who knows? Maybe I'll have to have surgery. Maybe the eye will be lost. Tomorrow is Sunday! How will I preach in my half-blind condition? How could this happen? I didn't feel anything!" I was sure I detected a growing deterioration in my sight as we neared the cars!

All the while we walked, as others in our hunting party joined us, I told the story of my bizarre accident. Each time I rubbed my eye and blinked furiously, hoping to dislodge the irritant and restore my sight. Then, when we had finished our hike, as we all stood in a semicircle collectively mourning my misfortune, one of the guys looked closely at me and said, "Hey, your left lens is gone!"

Sure enough! When I fired the gun, the recoil must have bumped my glasses, knocking out the left lens. I never thought to check my glasses because I never felt the jolt. I just assumed something injured my eye. My friends helped me see the real problem and find the missing lens. I went home that day rejoicing. My sight had been "restored." To this day I both laugh and shudder. I laugh at how "blind" I was to my real problem, and I shudder to think what would have happened if I'd been alone. Without friends I would not have left the field "seeing." Indeed, when it comes to "seeing" the way of holiness and "walking" in it, we need each other.

JESUS IN COMMUNITY

Jesus demonstrated our critical need for one another in the family of God. If ever there could be a spiritual Lone Ranger, you'd think the Son of God would qualify. Yet He sought and cherished community. One reason He called the twelve disciples was so that they would be "with Him" (Mark 3:14). The whole of Jesus' public life and ministry flowed out of the fellowship He established with these twelve. Yes, Jesus was starting the church and training His followers for their ministry after

He left, but He was also modeling the need we all have for community. And, because Jesus was human as well as divine, I think He was also satisfying His own need for fellowship.

Jesus cared deeply for all people, but He showed a special fondness for His twelve disciples, regarding them as family (see Mark 3:31-35). Even more, He seemed to rely on three of them—Peter, James, and John—as an inner circle of fellowship where the sharing was more intimate. Once, Jesus responded to the call to care for the dying daughter of Jairus, a ruler of the synagogue, and before He arrived at the home the child had died. "Don't be afraid, just believe," Jesus said. Dead or alive, Jesus would save this little girl. But He took with Him only Peter, James, and John to share in the joy of raising the child from the dead and restoring her to her parents (Mark 5:37-43).

Another time the same three accompanied Jesus to the top of a "high mountain," and witnessed an unforgettable display of glory. They also learned that paying attention to Jesus took priority over savoring the "mountaintop experience," and that future glory could be found only by following their Master (Mark 9:2-10).

You may think Jesus was just giving special attention to His star pupils, as any good teacher would. Yet, look to the night before His crucifixion when the three once again played an important role. In the Garden of Gethsemane, Jesus asked all the disciples, "Sit here while I pray." Then, He took Peter, James, and John along with Him and in their presence "began to be deeply distressed and troubled." He told them, "My soul is overwhelmed with sorrow to the point of death," and asked them to stay and keep watch as He went on farther to pray alone (Mark 14:32-34).

These events show us that Jesus was no Lone Ranger. He gathered a community and maintained it to the end. And He relied on this community, especially His three closest disciples, in His hour of greatest need. No doubt the denials and desertion of this fellowship deepened the pain of His saving work.

Jesus did not regard community—the family of God's people—as a mere option. Indeed, community stands at the heart of God's plan for His people. Apart from this fellowship, we simply cannot become who He calls us to be.

It is not surprising that the early church developed a rich and dynamic fellowship. Jesus told His disciples to await the promised Holy Spirit and they did, together. "They stayed continually at the temple, praising God" (Luke 24:53). "When the day of Pentecost came, they were all together in one place" (Acts 2:1). The Spirit's invasion of their lives was corporate as well as individual. In fact, the most powerful feature of the early church's witness seemed to be their fellowship!

> They devoted themselves to the apostles' teaching and to the fellowship, to the breaking of bread and to prayer. Everyone was filled with awe, and many wonders and miraculous signs were done by the apostles. All the believers were together and had everything in common. Selling their possessions and goods, they gave to anyone as he had need. Every day they continued to meet together in the temple courts. They broke bread in their homes and ate together with glad and sincere hearts, praising God and enjoying the favor of all the people. And the Lord added to their number daily those who were being saved (Acts 2:42-47).

Clearly, the church became the unique people of God because God's Spirit created a community to which others were drawn, in which they were formed, and from which they invaded the world as witnesses. In fact, the community *itself* proved nearly irresistible in its attraction to unbelievers.

THE BODY OF CHRIST

The whole New Testament speaks with one voice about the importance of community. God nurtures and matures the life of His people when they are in deep, loving relationships with one another. The most famous New Testament imagery for the church—the human body—makes this point powerfully.

> The body is a unit, though it is made up of many parts; and though all its parts are many, they form one body. So it is with Christ. For we were all baptized by one Spirit into one body—whether Jews or Greeks, slave or free—and we were all given the one Spirit to drink.
>
> Now the body is not made up of one part but of many. If the foot should say, "Because I am not a hand, I do not belong to the body," it would not for that reason cease to be part of the body. And if the ear should say, "Because I am not an eye, I do not belong to the body," it would not for that reason cease to be part of the body. If the whole body were an eye, where would the sense of hearing be? If the whole body were an ear, where would the sense of smell be? But in fact God has arranged the parts in the body, every one of them, just as He wanted them to be. If they were all one part, where would the body be? As it is, there are many parts, but one body.

The eye cannot say to the hand, "I don't need you!" And the head cannot say to the feet, "I don't need you!" On the contrary, those parts of the body that seem to be weaker are indispensable, and the parts that we think are less honorable we treat with special honor. And the parts that are unpresentable are treated with special modesty, while our presentable parts need no special treatment. But God has combined the members of the body and has given greater honor to the parts that lacked it, so that there should be no division in the body, but that its parts should have equal concern for each other. If one part suffers, every part suffers with it; if one part is honored, every part rejoices with it (1 Corinthians 12:12-26).

Just as each of us has one body with many members, and these members do not all have the same function, so in Christ we who are many form one body, and each member belongs to all the others (Romans 12:4-5).

It was He who gave some to be apostles, some to be prophets, some to be evangelists, and some to be pastors and teachers, to prepare God's people for works of service, so that the body of Christ may be built up until we all reach unity in the faith and in the knowledge of the Son of God and become mature, attaining to the whole measure of the fullness of Christ.

Then we will no longer be infants, tossed back and forth by the waves, and blown here and there by every wind of teaching and by the cunning and craftiness of men in their deceitful scheming. Instead, speaking the truth in love, we will in all things grow up into Him who is the Head, that is, Christ. From Him the whole body, joined and held together by every supporting ligament, grows and builds itself up in love, as each part does its work (Ephesians 4:11-16).

Just as it is impossible to have live body parts without a living body, so it is impossible for individual followers of Jesus to thrive in isolation from other followers. How grotesque it would be to see an eyeball rolling around "at will" with no connection to a head or body. Or, to observe a hand or leg detached from arm or hip! Each of us needs the Body—the community or family of God—to be alive and well as the holy people of God. Within the fellowship we see clearly who we are and how we may do God's will. Likewise, within the fellowship we grow and become like Jesus. The Scriptures offer no hint that any of this can happen apart from community, but they do promise that within the community, God's Spirit will empower His people to follow Jesus consistently and convincingly in the world.

GOD CREATES THE COMMUNITY WE NEED

Holiness calls for community, but not just any community. Not just any gathering of warm bodies will do! Often a church "community" or "fellowship" turns out to be a collaboration of like-minded people. Or, if not like-minded, alike in some other way—ethnically, socially, economically. What binds them together are their similarities.

But being in a group of people just like we are may, in fact, only encourage individualism. Suppose I gather some people who think and act the way I do. Then, when we're together we discover we share many of the same tastes and preferences (surprise, surprise!). We're so comfortable and feel blessed because we're so at home with one another. Of course, others are welcome to join us, but we notice that only people like us seem interested. And, of the interested, just a few ever actually join our group. What I've just described is what many a church has become—a group of folk bound together by their similarities. Belonging to such a group reinforces those characteristic similarities and encourages us to be satisfied just the way we are. But, underneath the similarities may hide all manner of things that never see the light of day because they are our unique problems and hang-ups and growing edges.

In a community bound together by similarity, it isn't safe to be different or unique. When differences surface, the group usually offers two options: resolve the differences so that you once again fit in, or leave. A community formed primarily on the basis of similarity tends to reinforce its members' self-centeredness and individualism. This kind of community will not tolerate the deep sharing that helps us become like Jesus.

We cannot simply decide to form a community whose members learn how to walk like Jesus. God alone can create the community we need. Our natural families help us understand this point. We don't decide who our families will be. Nobody asked me if I preferred to have only brothers and no sisters in my family of origin. I had nothing to do with the makeup of the family. Others composed the family and then put me in it. Likewise, a couple does not decide what sort of baby they will have— at least not yet! Their family comes into being as a creative, surprising miracle.

That's the way it works with the spiritual community or family we need as the people of God. God *cre-*

ates the community independent of human wisdom or power. Once we are born into the family of God, we find ourselves members of a community *He* has created.

Actually, God designs the church of Jesus Christ as an odd assortment of people. Within the community *He* creates, there are people who would probably never get together on their own. Consider some examples from the Scriptures.

On the Day of Pentecost, the Holy Spirit invaded the lives of Jesus' first followers and made them a large church—in excess of 3,000 people. But from the beginning, the church created by the Spirit included all sorts of people. We know that in the Pentecost congregation were people from most parts of the known world (see Acts 2:8-11). While most of them eventually returned to native soil, they still experienced a fellowship in the Spirit unlike any other fellowship they had known. And, in time, the movement of the Spirit crossed every cultural and social barrier and created family, even among those who had been bitter enemies. The community of God's people could not be explained in sociological or demographic terms. God was creating a community that would help His people learn to walk as Jesus walked.

Paul concludes his letter to the Romans by greeting a number of acquaintances. The names may strike us as strange, but studying the names of Paul's friends and the things he says about them reveals what a miracle God performs in creating community. Scholars tell us that these names suggest a group including male and female, slave and free, wealthy and poor, professional and laborer, urban and rural. This community has people of every social and economic stripe. Even more astounding, Paul describes this wide range of people with family terms, using words like sister, brother, beloved, kinsmen, mother. Then, he says these people relate to one another in ways ordinarily reserved only for family members. They risk their necks for each other (Romans 16:3-4). Or, they greet one another with a holy kiss, affection much too intimate for non-family. In other words, in the community God creates, you find people you'd never expect to be together in a family.

This still happens today. We have seen it, if indeed we have experienced the church as a community created by God.

When I was in graduate school my program of study put me together with six other persons—a U.S. Presbyterian, a Latin American Presbyterian, a Lutheran, a Canadian Mennonite, a Free Methodist, and a Roman Catholic. I cannot imagine any other set of circumstances that would have brought all of us together, but over time our association became a fellowship. Our common commitments to Jesus and the Scriptures drew us together. That fellowship, I'm convinced, was a creation of God, for only He could have given us the sense of family we enjoyed in those years, and from which each of us greatly benefited.

In the summer of 1993 my wife and I went on a short-term mission to South Africa. Over a five-week period we found ourselves members of a white minority who were warmly embraced by our brothers and sisters in South Africa. Time and again, despite the differences between us, we experienced a harmony of spirit and depth of sharing that surprised but delighted us. And the community God created among us challenged us and led us to change. One of these changes for me involved my preconceived notions about worship. It's hard to be rhythmically impaired amidst happy dancing Africans at worship. Before I left their fellowship even *I* was moving to the cadence of the African worship songs. My awkward attempts were not simply an effort to fit in, but expressed a freedom of worship I'd never known before. And though my performance was certainly laughable, I believe the Father smiled, much the way I smiled at the sight of my babies' first wobbly steps.

But we don't have to go somewhere exotic to recognize the miraculous character of the community God creates and we need. In most congregations you can see how God has brought together an unusual assortment of people. I've had the privilege of pastoring churches where the wealthy and the impoverished sit in the same pew Sunday after Sunday, where young people actually listen to and like old people, where farmers and professors have coffee together because they enjoy each other's company, where businesswomen and homemakers bear one another's burdens, where Republicans and Democrats work as partners in ministry, to name only a few of the common connections.

How do we explain these connections that make community? I know only one answer—God is at work creating a new people, His family. That He uses the most unlikely combinations witnesses to God's power. It also witnesses to God's plan. In the community He creates among us, we demonstrate God's will for all people. The barriers that separate us from God and from other people collapse. The fear that makes people suspicious and hateful has been cast out. And the selfishness that corrupts relationships of all people has been overcome. For in *this* kind of community, we who were made in God's image actually begin to look and live like Jesus. Spiritually speaking, we learn to "walk."

How Does God Create Community?

To answer this question is a bit like answering, "Where do babies come from?" Even though we have a scientific explanation, when it's all said and done, there remains an element of mystery. When a baby takes the first gasp of air and cries, most observers of the birth feel they've witnessed a miracle! The community God creates and we need qualifies for miracle status as well. And how do you explain a miracle?

■ Perhaps the best place to begin is simply to acknowledge God's creativity. In the beginning He created the universe out of nothing. That fact should settle once for all the question whether God can create the community we need, for when He created the first human beings, He made them for each other. God's statement, "It is not good for the man to be alone. I will make a helper suitable for him," (Genesis 2:18) was not only a reference to marriage. God was affirming the communal nature of all human beings. In the very beginning we were made to be our "brother's keeper" under the loving lordship of our God. And when sin disrupted everything, including our ability to relate to

one another, God's saving plan envisioned total restoration or re-creation, including the community so important to our well-being.

Therefore, in Christ's work to save us, we expect
God to set us right not only with Himself, but also with
other people. In truth, our relationships with God and
with others are so connected that the Scriptures often
describe them as two sides of the same coin. I think
that's the best way to understand Jesus' saying, "If you
forgive men when they sin against you, your heavenly
Father will also forgive you. But if you do not forgive
men their sins, your Father will not forgive your sins"
(Matthew 6:14-15). He's not suggesting that we win God's
forgiveness by forgiving others. Rather, God's love which
restores our relationship with Him also restores our relationships with others. Similarly, John writes:

> We love because He first loved us. If anyone
> says, "I love God," yet hates his brother, he is a
> liar. For anyone who does not love his brother,
> whom he has seen, cannot love God, whom he
> has not seen. And He has given us this com-
> mand: whoever loves God must also love his
> brother (1 John 4:19-21).

God's creative and saving love works both verti-
cally, between God and us, and horizontally, between
us and others. Community, therefore, is part and parcel
of God's plan of salvation for all people. And, the whole
plan of salvation works through Jesus by the power of
the Holy Spirit.

■ God creates community *through Jesus*, His Son.
Certainly that happened among the first disciples. Jesus
issued the call, "Follow Me," and a few fishermen, a tax
collector, a political activist, and several other types be-

came a community. They were an odd assortment, but they were united in their common response to Jesus' call and their commitment to follow. At the center of the community God creates, and we need, stands Jesus as Savior and Lord. Through commitment to Him and His ways, God creates a community.

Paul made this point to the Ephesian church. The work of Jesus in His cross and resurrection not only brings people from death to life individually (see Ephesians 2:1-10), but also unleashes power to tear down the walls of hostility that once separated bitter enemies—Jews and Gentiles.

> Therefore, remember that formerly you who are Gentiles by birth and called "uncircumcised" by those who call themselves "the circumcision" (that done in the body by the hands of men)—remember that at that time you were separate from Christ, excluded from citizenship in Israel and foreigners to the covenants of the promise, without hope and without God in the world. But now in Christ Jesus you who once were far away have been brought near through the blood of Christ.
>
> For He Himself is our peace, who has made the two one and has destroyed the barrier, the dividing wall of hostility, by abolishing in His flesh the law with its commandments and regulations. His purpose was to create in Himself one new man out of the two, thus making peace, and in this one body to reconcile both of them to God through the cross, by which He put to death their hostility. He came and preached peace to you who were far away and peace to those who were near. For through Him we both have access to the Father by one Spirit.

Consequently, you are no longer foreigners and aliens, but fellow citizens with God's people and members of God's household (Ephesians 2:11-19).

As I read Paul's words, I realize that we preachers are often guilty of sharing only half of the good news. We boldly proclaim Christ's death on the cross as God's great reconciling work. "No matter how bad you've been and no matter how you've treated God in the past, Jesus' death will make peace with God. Accept the gospel and enjoy a loving relationship with God as a gift!"

But that's only half the good news. Shouldn't we also declare that Christ's death on the cross tears down walls of hatred and bitterness that divide us from others? And, on the basis of God's Word, shouldn't we expect that Jesus will mend our broken relationships with others as much as we expect Him to mend our relationship with God? I think so.

How does God create the community we need? Part of the answer is that He has already done it, in the death and resurrection of Jesus. "He *is* our peace," Paul says. Peace with others comes as a gift from God just as peace with God. We must recognize and receive this facet of Jesus' saving work. Then, we must proclaim it as good news and expect that God will make it so.

■ But how does God make it so? God works through Jesus *by the power of the Holy Spirit*. As in every aspect of God's saving work, the Spirit applies the grace of God and accomplishes the will of God in our lives. On the Day of Pentecost when the Holy Spirit came, He brought individuals into right relationship with God and with one another. Some scholars suggest that Pentecost was a kind of reversal of the Tower of Babel episode in the Old Testament. You'll recall that people of that day

178

determined to make a name for themselves by building a tower into heaven. They formed a community based on arrogance and disdain for God. It was a community God could not tolerate, and He confused their languages. Since they could no longer communicate, they scattered across the face of the earth (see Genesis 11:1-9).

At Pentecost God's Spirit filled the followers of Jesus and gave them ability to communicate the good news. This Spirit-empowered communication led to community. People from across the face of the earth, in Jerusalem for the Feast, heard the good news and were drawn to accept it. In accepting the good news they were also drawn to accept one another. God created the community we need by the power of the Holy Spirit (see Acts 2).

Actually, the story of Acts gives us an account of how the Spirit of God expanded this very community from one place to another, gathering a diverse people into one holy fellowship. In each phase of the expansion, God created community by the Spirit's power. When questions arose about whether certain types of people really belonged to the people of God, the Spirit's work in their lives validated them as members of the community (see Acts 10:44-48; 11:15-18; 15:8-11; 19:1-17).

How does God create community? If the work of Jesus makes community a gift God offers to all, the work of God's Spirit activates this gift among people. "For we were all baptized by one Spirit into one body— whether Jews or Greeks, slave or free—and we were all given the one Spirit to drink" (1 Corinthians 12:13). By the Spirit's power there is peace and oneness among the people of God.

From the teachings of Scripture, we are driven to several conclusions. First, we should expect community, a deep family-style fellowship, among us. If we preach and teach the whole gospel, peace and unity should follow as a matter of course. Second, if such fellowship does not exist, then something has gone wrong at the point of communicating or accepting the gospel. Assuming God remains true to His plan seen so clearly in His Word, a lack of community signals a failure to accept the whole gospel message. Third, the remedy for a deficient fellowship is simple—revisit the good news of Jesus, understand it fully, and embrace it entirely. Then, God will work His plan, creating the community we need.

THE IMPORTANCE OF LOVE

But, once again, *how* will this happen among *us?* How does God work with each of us so that together we become a community? I'm convinced that we're more than halfway there when we realize that God creates community through Jesus by the power of the Holy Spirit, and that this is a miracle.

The miracle of community begins in our individual hearts. God must first give us the capacity, that is, empower us for the love that leads to community. Peter describes it this way, "You have purified yourselves by obeying the truth so that you have sincere love for your brothers" (1 Peter 1:22). Notice the words "so that." They tell us that "obeying the truth" purifies us and results in a sincere love for others. Peter clarifies in the next verses. "For you have been born again, not of perishable seed, but of imperishable, through the living and enduring Word of God ... the Word that was preached to you" (1 Peter 1:23-25).

On our own we cannot love as we need to. As we've seen in earlier chapters, though we were made to reflect God's likeness and love, sin has taught us to look after "number one." By nature we become individual-ists—either proud of our independence and personal achievements or bitter and broken over our failures and needs. (Probably a mixture of both.) Apart from God's help, we cannot reach out to God or others as we were made to do. Someone must save us from ourselves and our selfish preoccupations. Someone must give us a new life capable of deep love for God and others. Of course, Someone has—Jesus rescues us from our self-centeredness.

When we say, "Yes, I want the life God offers," God gives us a new life. It's like being born all over again. And Peter says that our "yes" to God purifies us and gives us the ability to love others sincerely and deeply. Paul put it like this, "God has poured out His love into our hearts by the Holy Spirit, whom He has given us" (Romans 5:5). For the first time, we become people able to reflect God's likeness and love. And, for the first time, the community we need comes within reach, through Jesus' work and by the power of the Holy Spirit.

God then expects us to use the capacity for love He's given us. The fact is that we can have the ability and not use it, or stop using it. Just because we *can* love, doesn't mean we *will*. At the root of every broken relationship and community lies a failure to love.

Indeed, the command to love is *the* supreme com-mand Jesus gave His followers. "A new command I give you; Love one another. As I have loved you, so you must love one another. By this all men will know that you are My disciples, if you love one another" (John 13:34-35). Now that you are armed with the capacity to love, Jesus says, "Love! Love the way I have loved you. Love one another so that others will know you belong to Me."

How will love flow from one to another in the community God creates? Consider the "one another" statements in the New Testament, statements that show us love in action.

As I have loved you, so you must love one another (John 13:35; 15:12, 17).

Be devoted to one another in brotherly love. Honor one another above yourselves (Romans 12:10).

Live in harmony with one another. Do not be proud, but be willing to associate with people of low position. Don't be conceited (Romans 12:16).

Let no debt remain outstanding, except the continuing debt to love one another (Romans 13:8).

Let us stop passing judgment on one another. Instead, make up your mind not to put any stumbling block or obstacle in your brother's way (Romans 14:13).

Accept one another, then, just as Christ accepted you (Romans 15:7).

You yourselves are full of goodness, complete in knowledge and competent to instruct one another (Romans 15:14).

I appeal to you, brothers, in the name of our Lord Jesus Christ, that all of you agree with one another so that there may be no divisions among you and that you may be perfectly united in mind and thought (1 Corinthians 1:10).

You ... were called to freedom. But do not use your freedom to indulge the sinful nature; rather, serve one another in love (Galatians 5:13).

Be completely humble and gentle; be patient, bearing with one another in love (Ephesians 4:2).

Be kind and compassionate with one another, forgiving each other, just as in Christ God forgave you (Ephesians 4:32).

Speak to one another with psalms, hymns, and spiritual songs (Ephesians 5:19).

Submit to one another out of reverence for Christ (Ephesians 5:21).

Let the word of Christ dwell in you richly as you teach and admonish one another with all wisdom (Colossians 3:16).

Therefore encourage one another and build each other up (1 Thessalonians 5:11; Hebrews 3:13).

Let us consider how we may spur one another on toward love and good deeds. Let us not give up meeting together, as some are in the habit of doing, but let us encourage one another (Hebrews 10:24-25).

Offer hospitality to one another without grumbling (1 Peter 4:9).

Clothe yourselves with humility toward one another, because, "God opposes the proud but gives grace to the humble" (1 Peter 5:5).

As you can see, God's Word repeatedly commands us to "love one another," and offers extensive commentary on how this will shape our behaviors and attitudes. All of these commands *assume* the capacity to love that

God gives each of us when we say "Yes" to Him and begin to follow Jesus. Now that we are able, we must love one another. And, if we will use the Spirit-given ability to love, who can doubt that we will enjoy a wonderful fellowship!

The command to love has both a positive and negative expression. If we love, *we will do* certain things. Likewise, if we love, *we will not do* certain other things. In general, we will not do or think or say anything contrary to love. But we can be more specific, because the Bible is.

Peter, for example, expresses a positive command. Since the truth has cleansed you of selfishness so that you *may* love, now "love one another deeply, from the heart" (1 Peter 1:22). The language Peter uses carries great intensity. He's really urging his readers to become a community of "intensive care." But what does that mean?

He answers by expressing a negative command or prohibition. Have nothing to do with unloving attitudes and words among us. I like how the *Contemporary English Version* puts it: "Stop being hateful!" (1 Peter 2:1). That we have the capacity to love as Jesus did doesn't mean we are no longer able to hate and become bitter. These destructive emotions can get hold of us. We must recognize this danger when we experience disappointment in others, as we certainly will, and allow no place for hatred or bitterness.

Peter continues, "Quit trying to fool people, and start being sincere. Don't be jealous or say cruel things about others" (1 Peter 2:1, CEV). We've all felt tempted to be someone other than we are, to pretend rather than be real. We also sometimes compare ourselves with others in the community. As a result, we may feel superior to those less fortunate and inferior to those more fortunate. The result can be either pride or jealousy. Often the tongue becomes the weapon of choice to cut people down to size! But none of this can keep company with love. God's Word says to "get rid" of every trace of such things.

Because we have the *capacity* to love, we *can* be free of these negative attitudes and can avoid acting and speaking contrary to love. That's a tall order, you say. Indeed, but this is God's work through Jesus and by the power of the Holy Spirit. His mighty work forms the basis for our consistently loving relationships with one another.

Perhaps that's the way it *should* work, you're thinking. But what happens when we fail to love, when we give in to temptation and say or do something unloving, or when others do? Even then the capacity for love can show us the way. Remember the many times when the "one anothers" of the New Testament stress forgiveness, bearing with one another, and admonishing one another? There is good reason for this emphasis: in any human community there will be failure. But in the community God creates, no failure is beyond recovery.

Peter expresses this beautifully when he says, "Love each other deeply, because love covers a multitude of sins" (1 Peter 4:8). Don't misunderstand, love doesn't condone or excuse sin. Instead, love creates community where it's okay to be human—to make mistakes, to fail, even to sin. It's a community where it's okay to be human, but not okay to be unforgiving. Love creates a community where forgiveness may be sought and received. Again, that doesn't lead to indulgence, but to accountability, owning up to wrong, restoration to fellowship, and transformation. Love forgives and makes people new.

WILL WE LIVE IN COMMUNITY?

We need the community that only God can create. And, it's simpler than we might think, though not easy. The full gospel proclaims a radical and comprehensive reconciliation—both with God and with others. Jesus died and rose again, and His finished work provides the foundation for community. No barrier to the sharing we need with others can stand in the face of what Jesus has already accomplished. He is our peace (Ephesians 2:17). My kids would say, "It's a done deal!"

God's Holy Spirit creates community on the foundation of Jesus' work. Wherever people welcome the good news, committing themselves to Jesus as Savior and Lord, and are open to the Spirit's indwelling presence, community cannot help but happen. And, what a community! It made the earliest believers so faithful to Jesus that not even martyrdom could shake them. It led them to care for each other's needs in ways that amazed the unbelieving world (see Acts 2:45-47; 32-35). It supported them when they faced harassment and persecution from the authorities (see, for example, Acts 4:23-31; 12:1-17). And it provided the powerful and positive peer pressure necessary for them to live out the gospel in radical ways. Apart from such community these early believers could not have survived as the holy people of God, much less thrive.

But this community God creates and we need is not a relic of the past. God's Spirit continues to activate the finished work of Jesus among people, creating community. For example, astonishing reports come out of China these days, estimating a network of faithful Christians numbering in the millions. Certainly one of the keys to this miraculous growth of the church is the close-knit fellowship of the house-churches. Despite unbelievable pressure and persecution from the government, God has used these fellowships to produce Christians who are a threat to worldly powers. This has happened in the twentieth century, but it sounds like first-century Christianity.

I recall my own first days in love with Jesus. The sharing and caring of comrades in faith was absolutely essential. Without their support, encouragement, and occasional rebuke, I'm not sure where I'd be today. Since those first days in faith, the most intense spiritual growth has always come through deep sharing and caring with the community God gave me. And, as a pastor, I hardly ever see people who are growing, becoming more and more like Jesus, and using their gifts for God and others, apart from vital connection with others.

Presently, one of my greatest joys as a pastor comes from watching the young adults in my church—senior high and college students, and even some middle schoolers. In chapter 10 I told you about several young people who came to know Jesus and suffered the misunderstanding of their parents, and worse. It's fair to say that they were won to Jesus in the first place by God's power at work in the fellowship of our young people. Then, when these new believers faced pressure to stop following Jesus, their new brothers and sisters held on to them. Literally, the power of love within their community kept them from renouncing Christ. But, even more, those tough times weathered with the help of the community actually strengthened them in the process. When the pressure let up, they were more committed to Christ's way than ever. Because the community held on to them in love, they gained a firmer grasp on the Lord. Again, it happened in the twentieth century, but it sounds like the first century to me!

I yearn for the whole church to know this same essential community. Without it the holy life and its deepest joys simply cannot be lived and known. I remind you, the work is done—Jesus has laid the foundation and the Spirit of God wants to make it real for us. If we have begun to walk with Jesus, you and I have the capacity to love. The only question is what we will do with the command. *Will we love?*

I want to ask two questions to urge you toward application of the truth. First, is there anything that keeps you from loving as Jesus loved? Ask the question sincerely and prayerfully. It's a question God will not leave unanswered. If He points out anything, let His Spirit cleanse the barrier away. Let Him give you full capacity to love.

Second, are you in community with others right now? I'm not asking only if you go to church or if you are faithful in devotional or service activities. Rather, are there some folks with whom you share deeply and regularly—who know you, who support you in living like Jesus, who can ask you the tough questions, people for whom you can do the same? God's Word assures us that without such people we will never find our proper stride on the way of holiness. His Word also assures us that He will provide the community we need. It is His will.

God is at work to create the community we need, and in my heart's eye, I see God raising up a new generation of Christians:

- *people* overwhelmed by who God shows Himself to be in Jesus, barely able to believe how deeply God loves them and unable to help but love Him in return;
- *people* whose sense of God's undeserved for-

giveness prompts a reflex response back to God and to others who deserve God's love no more than they do and to whom it is no less offered;

- *people* who, therefore, hunger and thirst for more of God and whose appetite God satisfies;
- *people* who find themselves by losing themselves in Jesus, who find themselves now oriented to God, others, and self the way Jesus was;
- *people* whose dependence on God leads them to value and depend on the family God gives them in Jesus, who discover how deeply they need this family to continue following Jesus— even when it means costly sacrifice, service, and suffering in order to do what Jesus would do;
- *people* who know *they* could never be or do as God calls them, and yet they *are* and they *do*, because God empowers them by His Spirit;
- *people* whose former brokenness is clearly on the mend, whose relationships reveal a beauty and attractiveness that many of the love-starved and sin-stained folk around them will find irresistible.

It seems right to think that among such people as these, consumer-oriented Christians stand a good chance of seeing how trivial their pursuits are when compared to following Jesus. Some of them may grow passionate about being all God calls them to be, and begin having the time of their lives.

It also seems right to think that among such holy people, the broken, addicted, and deceived of our world will see the true way of life with its promise of healing, freedom, and peace. And, no doubt, some of them will become brand new persons!

Of course, reality falls short of what my heart's

eye can envision. But it falls short only because God and the world still wait for a people to hear God's call and receive God's empowering to be like Jesus. God and the world wait for people like us to pray, along with the songwriter:

> Spirit of God, descend upon my heart:
> Wean it from earth, thro' all its pulses move.
> Stoop to my weakness, mighty as Thou art,
> And make me love Thee as I ought to love.
>
> Hast Thou not bid us love Thee, God and King?
> All, all Thine own—soul, heart and strength and mind.
> I see Thy cross—there teach my heart to cling;
> O let me seek Thee, and O let me find.
>
> Teach me to feel that Thou art always nigh;
> Teach me the struggles of the soul to bear—
> To check the rising doubt, the rebel sigh;
> Teach me the patience of unanswered prayer.
>
> Teach me to love Thee as Thine angels love,
> One holy passion filling all my frame:
> The baptism of the heav'n-descended Dove—
> My heart an altar and Thy love the flame.
>
> Amen.[1]

CHAPTER ONE
1. Margaret Wolfe Hungerford, *Molly Brown*, 1878.
2. "Pastor's Weekly Briefing," Focus on the Family, January 18, 1997.
3. Robert W. Funk, Brandon S. Scott, James R. Butts, *The Parables of Jesus: Jesus Seminar Red Letter Edition*, Sonoma, California: Polebridge Press, 1988.

CHAPTER FOUR
1. Anonymous, *The Hymnal for Worship and Celebration*, Irving, Texas: Word Music, 1989, 745.

CHAPTER SIX
1. Anne Gearan, "From War to Peace," Wichita *Eagle*, May 3, 1997.

CHAPTER EIGHT
1. Doug Nichols, "Evangelism," *Leadership*, Spring 1994, 94.
2. Kevin Miller, "From the Editor," *Leadership*, Winter 1996, 3.

CHAPTER NINE
1. Quoted by John Stott, *The Contemporary Christian*, Downers Grove, Illinois: Inter Varsity Press, 1992, 242.

CHAPTER TEN
1. Letter from Dr. Larry Houck, General Director of World Missions, Free Methodist Church, August 27, 1997.
2. Ralph Kinney Bennet, "The Global War on Christians," *Reader's Digest*, August 1997, 51.

CHAPTER TWELVE
1. George Croly, "Spirit of God, Descend Upon My Heart," *The Hymnal for Worship and Celebration*, 249.

Betty, Mike C.,
Forths, Core,